You can eat well, even healthy, on a lo[...] 7/12
family can do it, because we do it!—fro[...]

"Practical and easy to read. I recommend [Rh[...]
ods to anyone wanting to eat better for less." MAR 1 0 2005
      —Mary Hunt, editor of *Cheapsk[...]*
      and author of *The Best of C[...]*
      The Cheapsk 6/23

"If feeding your family for only $50 a week se[...]
dream, wake up and meet Rhonda Barfield."
    —Sarah Casey Newman, Food Columnist,

Rhonda Barfield and her six member family hav[...]
developed, tested, and used methods for cu[...]
budget, keeping good nutrition a priority! She
FEED YOUR FAMILY FOR $12 A DAY.

You'll learn:
- how to identify the excuses you're using
  change them into simple reasons *to do it*
- how to shop smart at supermarkets and g[...]
  even more with coupons, refunding, and
- how to get the most out of food cooperat[...]
- how to save time and cook a whole month's worth of meals—in
  one day
- Plus dozens of delicious and healthy low-cost recipes, complete
  with nutritional analyses, and much, much more, to help you
  FEED YOUR FAMILY FOR $12 A DAY.

FEED YOUR FAMILY
FOR $12 A DAY

A Complete Guide to Nutritious, Delicious Meals for Less Money

RHONDA BARFIELD

CITADEL PRESS
Kensington Publishing Corp.
www.kensingtonbooks.com

CITADEL PRESS BOOKS are published by

Kensington Publishing Corp.
850 Third Avenue
New York, NY 10022

Copyright © 1996, 2002 Rhonda Barfield

All Kensington titles, imprints, and distributed lines are available at special quantity discounts for bulk purchases for sales promotions, premiums, fund-raising, educational, or institutional use. Special book excerpts or customized printings can also be created to fit specific needs. For details, write or phone the office of the Kensington special sales manager: Kensington Publishing Corp., 850 Third Avenue, New York, NY 10022, attn: Special Sales Department, phone 1-800-221-2647.

Citadel Press and the Citadel Logo are trademarks of Kensington Publishing Corp.

The first edition of this book was published in 1996 and entitled *Eat Healthy for $50 a Week*. This is a revised and updated edition.

First printing: June 2002

10 9 8 7 6 5 4 3 2 1

Printed in the United States of America

Library of Congress Control Number: 2001099893

ISBN 0-806-52355-7

CONTENTS

Find out why the Barfields cut their spending on groceries and how that savings helped them to realize a dream in their lives. Read about the family's conversion to healthier eating and the reasons behind the change. Discover how, in spite of the spiraling cost of providing food for growing children, you can feed your family for $12 a day. Survey a summary of this book's contents.

Learn Rhonda's methods for saving money at the store • Check out her shopping list • Read the menu plans that follow.

Save Money on What You Buy (Meats; Dairy Foods; Name Brand Goods; Produce; Breads and Grains) • Bulk Buy from Membership Warehouse Clubs • Try the Pantry Principle™ • Use Coupons • Do Refunding • Check Out Alternative Stores (Produce Stands; Pick-Your-Own Places; Farmers' Markets; Dairies; Scratch-and-Dent Stores; Health Food Stores; Bakery Outlets)

Belong to a Cooperative • Barter (National Commercial Exchange; SHARE) • Get Organized (Meal Plan; Do Once-a-Month Cooking;

Mega-Cook®; Use Leftovers; Try the 24-Hour-in-Advance Meal Plan; Do 15-Minute Cooking) • Make or Cook Your Own (Meats and Other Proteins; Dairy Foods; Breads, Grains, and Cereals; Other Foods; Drinks) • Garden (Cooperative Extension Services; Gardening Books and Publications; Garden Clubs) • Preserve Your Food (Freezing; Canning) • Glean • Benefit from Government Programs • Eat Sensibly

ACKNOWLEDGMENTS

My sincere thanks go to Nancy Castleman, Marc Eisenson, Marcy Ross, Jackie Iglehart, Candace Magruder, and Anneliese Thomas for their thorough proofreading and constructive criticism of many passages in this text. Toni Lopopolo, my agent, deserves credit for selling the manuscript, and Richard Ember, my editor, for overseeing this project.

Carol Schlitt, Extension Educator of Nutrition and Wellness at the University of Illinois Cooperative Extension Service, did me the great favor of nutritionally analyzing all my recipes at no cost; I am most grateful. JoAnn Knapp, Sally Davis, and Jan Kent researched a number of recipes and shared them freely. Many others contributed by offering expert advice and information. I appreciate all the loving input.

Thank you, Mother, and mother-in-law Marilyn, for some wonderful recipes and cooking tips through the years. I am always inspired by your good examples of thriftiness.

I'm especially grateful to my husband and dearest friend, Michael, for encouragement, computer support, and long Monopoly games with our children. Thank you, too, Eric, Christian, Lisa, and Mary, for putting up with Mom on the days when I was absorbed in writing, and you kept busy elsewhere.

Feed Your Family for $12 a Day is dedicated to those who want to eat good, nutritious foods, yet save back extra cash—as we did—in order to realize dreams in their lives.

INTRODUCTION

Welcome to *Feed Your Family for $12 a Day*

Perhaps you've heard of my original book, *Eat Well for $50 a Week*, and then the rewrite, *Eat Healthy for $50 a Week*. You may even know the story behind these books: how, several years ago, my family of six cut our grocery bill in half, from almost $100 to $50 a week, in order to help bail us out of both a financial crisis and a bad neighborhood.

Throughout our twenty-eight years of marriage, my husband, Michael, and I have never made much money. Michael is an artist, and my training and background are in music. Both of us broke the Unofficial Law of the Arts: Never marry an artist (or a musician) unless *you've* got a great-paying job. Still, though we've always been relatively poor, our lives have been good.

Several years ago the two of us began a financial tailspin. It started when we both quit our jobs in order to interview for better positions in other parts of the country. We had several good leads on employment and were sure we could move right into solid careers. But it didn't work out that way at all. As we traveled to West Virginia, North Carolina, and Florida, we charged food, car repairs, and interview expenses on credit cards. (We know now how foolish this was, but didn't think it was then.)

We were unemployed for nearly a year. Eventually I was hired to teach at a piano school and Michael freelanced in art. Then came children, four in six years. Michael went to work for a publishing company, but wasn't paid well. When my part-time, insurance company employer gave me an ultimatum—work full-time or be laid off—I chose to leave and stay home with the children. By that time, money was really tight.

In spite of serious financial problems, our lives were peaceful, at least for a while. Then our apartment complex began to deteriorate, and rapidly. In one year's time the area changed, as newcomers moved in and most others moved out. There were rumors of a crack house down the street, and burglaries everywhere. One night as we slept, someone nearly broke in through our bedroom window.

We wanted to leave but simply didn't have the money. Bringing in more cash was not a possibility at the time. And how could we ever afford the higher rent needed for a nice house in a better part of town? We analyzed our budget over and over again, trying to think of some way to squeeze out an extra $100 or more a month.

At last we decided to trim our food budget. It wasn't much, but by paring our spending from nearly $100 down to $50 a week, we were soon able to afford a lovely three-bedroom home with nearly four times the space of our cramped apartment. For $200 more a month (in additional rent and utilities), our family now lives comfortably and safely.

I think you can see how voluntarily limiting our food spending has made such a difference in our lives. By cutting our grocery bill in half, we now have something much more important to us than steaks and microwave dinners.

Still, saving money isn't everything. And now my story continues.

Several years ago, when Michael and I self-published *Eat Well for $50 a Week*, I was convinced that we really ate well. In reading through four weeks of "real-life menus" I recorded in my book, many agreed. A registered dietician looked over my meals and commented, "Although these menus may not exactly meet all the recommended dietary guidelines, when balancing budget, food preferences of children, and dietary considerations, they are adequate and realistic."

Others strongly disagreed. One nutrtional expert went so far as to say, "I find it hard to believe that any registered dietitian would approve of the way your family eats." And the worst part of it was this: If I could not demonstrate that we ate well on our budget, maybe nobody could eat well on a thrifty budget. Perhaps every family should make high spending on food a priority, and trim back in less important areas. If so, then I certainly had no business counseling others to cut their grocery budgets while undermining their good nutrition.

You can imagine how confused I felt. I had always believed my knowledge of proper nutrtion was, at least, better than average. Now I realized that I had much to learn. I began to read, whenever I could fit in a chapter or even a paragraph or two. I'm afraid I uncovered just enough information to confuse me even further.

I read, for example, that some authors advocated strict vegetarianism as a means of eating healthy. Some vegetarians recommended no dairy products; others did. Some experts insisted you must eat your foods in a certain order, such as fruit only in the mornings, fresh vegetables for lunch, etc. Some were adamant about serving only organic foods and whole grains. Some suggested no more than 30% fat in one's diet, while others demanded no more than 20%, or even 10%. Some recommended no sugar, or limited sugar, or honey, or sugar substitutes, or none of the above . . . and the list went on.

Even worse, none of these books seemed very kid friendly. Many of the recipes were incredibly complicated, overly exotic, or simply awful-sounding. I could have served them to my family, but I was sure the dishes would never be eaten. (Would your children gobble down artichoke hearts on a bed of vegetables?) The end result of my initial research discouraged me from trying to change anything in our diet. This was just too hard.

And then, gradually, I began to recognize some common themes of good nutrition in much of what I was reading. These themes were confirmed when a registered dietician at Barnes Hospital, here in St. Louis, did an overall analysis of my menus and recommended that my family improve our diet as follows:

1. Use fewer foods high in hidden fat.
2. Increase fruits and vegetables, including a good vitamin C source daily. (Recommended servings are three to five vegetables and two to four fruits daily.)
3. Increase low-fat dairy products as children need three servings daily.
4. Try to increase fiber content of menus with inclusion of more whole-grain breads, cereals, rice, and increased amounts of fruits and vegetables as previously suggested.
5. Possibly use more dried beans and other low-cost protein sources to enhance protein content of menus.

At last, I had some kind of tangible, reasonable goals to work toward. And now, the important question: Could I incorporate a healthier way of shopping and cooking into our lifestyle, one which my family would support, and still do it for $50 a week? I resolved to try. Over three years' time, we gradually made some changes in our diet. Here's how my family converted to a new way of eating.

1. We cut our consumption of red meat—and, in turn, much saturated fat—by two thirds. Instead, we eat more chicken, fish, and nearly vegetarian meals. I cook more nutritious, low-fat desserts, and eliminate most of the oil called for in many baked goods. I replace regular margarine, whenever possible, with reduced amounts of vegetable oil, and try to avoid excess fat altogether. We eat more baked and broiled—and very few fried—foods. We cut back on our consumption of high-fat snack foods like potato chips and cheese curls.
2. We try to eat at least "5 a day for better health," as the American Cancer Society recommends, referring to fruits and vegetables. We now buy primarily from a local produce stand, where we know produce is as fresh as possible. I serve most fruits and vegetables raw in order to better preserve nutrition.
3. We keep nonfat powdered milk on hand and mix extra portions into baked goods and other foods (like salmon croquettes) when possible, to increase the children's number of dairy servings.
4. I use oats in many of our baked goods, and/or oat flour, wheat germ, and whole-wheat flour. I buy and serve 100% whole-grain bread.
5. We have increased our weekly servings of beans, and plan to eat more in the future.

I might add that we've also cut our sugar content considerably, though this has been difficult. We've decided not to use many substitutes, just eat less sweeteners.

Overall, I think we've been successful in significantly improving our diet. We seem to go in cycles, first eating very healthy foods, then sliding toward less healthy ones, and finally, consuming a fair amount of junk along with the nutritious foods. Then we have a wake-up call and start all over again with healthier eating. We continue to try to cut back on fat and increase servings of fruits, vegetables, low-fat dairy products, whole grains, and beans. It isn't easy, sticking to a healthy diet. But I believe we're on solid middle ground, as far as nutritional theory goes.

And now for a third update. Since I wrote *Eat Healthy for $50 a Week*, food prices are up by perhaps 30% or more and $50 simply doesn't buy as much as it used to buy. We have now decided on a weekly spending limit of $80 to $90—about $12 a day—as a more reasonable budget for our family. I think you'll find this true for your family, too.

In addition to higher costs per item, our grocery bills have risen because our children have grown. Several years ago, $50 a week fed us comfortably when Eric was nine, Christian was eight, Lisa was six, and Mary was four. Now my children's ages are fifteen, fourteen, twelve, and ten. Eric is a serious weight lifter and requests certain foods, like ten cans of tuna in spring water, a couple of boxes of bran flakes cereal, and six cups of fat-free yogurt—per week. Both of the boys eat like horses. All four children are very tall (at fifteen, Eric is 6'4" and wears size 15 shoes) and active, and need a great deal of food to fill them up, sometimes as much as three times the amount we used to serve at meals. And when teens are hormonal or hungry, just like toddlers, they need a snack . . . now!

But they aren't toddlers, so I can no longer tell my offspring, "You will eat this." I find I must offer my young adults choices or face a confrontation over food—and personally, I think there are more important battles to choose. We have compromised in the area of breakfast foods, for example: I buy more boxed cereal now than in earlier years. And so the food bill goes up.

Still, in spite of challenges, there is hope. By using the principles in this book, you should be able to work out your own personal plan for drastically reducing your grocery bill.

How? In Chapter 1 and the Appendix you'll find shopping lists and three weeks of our new-and-improved menu plans, in order to give you a starting point for personalizing your own plans. Please keep in mind that my lists were never intended to be the Great Master Plans for Shopping and Cooking, far from it. Many of you may find my child-oriented meals pretty boring. For that reason, I have included recipes from other sources. You have to decide how you want to organize, shop, and cook for your family, and what works best for you. *Feed Your Family for $12 a Day* will give you the information and the tools needed to individualize your strategies, improve the quality of your food, and still save a significant amount of money.

My book will show you ways to cut costs on nearly every food item you buy, from fresh produce to chicken breasts to whole-grain breads. And if you're looking for overall strategies to help you save big, you'll find a crash course explaining bulk buying, couponing, refunding, cooperatives, bartering, getting organized, meal planning, making or cooking your own food, gardening, preserving food, and more. Chapters 2 and 3 tell you how to "beat the system," whether you do so at the store or elsewhere. The section on resources, newly updated, provides valuable information, addresses, Web sites, and phone numbers for more information.

Perhaps you've read all the theories behind saving on good food but can't understand how to really make it happen. You'll find help in Chapter 4, where a hypothetical family changes their lifestyle little by little, one or two changes a week, for fifty-two weeks of the year. The results are big savings on their food budget, and a healthier way of eating as well.

You may think you have a good excuse—from catering to demanding children to having very little time to cook—for spending lots of money on high-cost, low-nutrition convenience foods at the supermarket. If so, refer to Chapter 5. There may be an answer there for you. Or read the point-by-point checklist in Chapter 7, an overview of this book's ideas to help you save money on healthy groceries.

I enjoy cooking (usually), but between running a household, home schooling four children, and writing, I average an hour and a half a day for preparing food. I know how busy we all are. That's why you'll find my recipes in Chapter 6 to be mostly fast and easy, as well as healthy, dishes. Your family will like them, too.

Are you wondering if all this, whatever you decide to do, requires an incredible amount of time and energy? Not nearly as much as you might think. The hardest part is getting started, trying a number of strategies until you find what works best for your family.

All in all, I think I have some wonderfully helpful advice to share. I know there are many, many people who can benefit from the information in *Feed Your Family for $12 a Day*. Perhaps you're living from paycheck to paycheck, laid off, unemployed, or trying to survive on Social Security. Maybe you're a working parent who yearns to stay home with your children. You might need extra cash for a son's or daughter's college education, or a nicer home, or other dreams in your life. In addition, maybe you're now on a low-cholesterol diet, overweight, or concerned about possible heart disease or cancer. If so, I have good news: You can outline a healthy diet for yourself and your family, and you can implement it for less money than you probably imagine.

In fact, the grocery budget is a perfect place to start saving dollars. While it may not be possible to cut back immediately on house or car payments or other expenses, you can begin to economize on good food today. If you are a typical American family spending, say, $154 a week, scaling down to $84 is a $70 weekly savings, a $280 monthly savings, and a $3,640 yearly savings, all of it tax-free "income." That's a lot of cash.

So with all this said, why not begin to *Feed Your Family for $12 a Day*?

CHAPTER 1

Real-Life Shopping

Have you ever made a quick stop at the grocery store for milk and bread, and found yourself filling your cart—and emptying your pocketbook—instead? Of course you have; we all have. And that's how I used to do most of my shopping. I enjoyed rambling through the supermarket, choosing a few essential items, and splurging on anything else that looked appealing. When we implemented our $50-a-week food budget, I simply couldn't do that anymore: $50 plus impulse buying yielded two and a half bags of groceries, much of it items that were not even very nutritious. That was certainly not enough to feed a family of six well for a week.

Several years ago, I faced another challenge in trying to buy healthier foods. How could I increase our fruit and vegetable consumption without spending a fortune? Where could I get the best buys on whole-grain bread and chicken pieces? Which was cheaper, a membership warehouse club or a local supermarket?

Now my main challenge is finding reasonably healthy, lower-cost foods in large quantities, enough to fill up my growing children. I've had to take my own advice and thoroughly re-research the strategies mentioned in this and the next two chapters. Here are the guidelines I decided on many years ago (I still find them very helpful).

1. *Set a limit on spending.*

It's been my experience that if I allow myself $120, I spend that much just as easily as I spend $84, that is, $12 a day. Restricting my

1

outlay helps me to think creatively about possibilities. I have to carefully examine priorities. Do I really need to buy juice boxes for the
children, or expensive snack crackers? Is there a cheaper, healthier
substitute? What helps most is thinking of the budget as an adventure
rather than a toilsome burden. How much can I buy for $12 a day?—
this is my objective. It's a kind of game to try to get more for my
money each week.

Nobody says you should spend what I spend. You may actually
have to go lower, or you might find $100 to $125 or higher a much
more comfortable range. Limiting yourself is still important. It makes
you feel in control of your budget and forces you to use money
wisely.

2. *Compare prices.*

I have about 100 prices from my favorite store memorized, not because I planned to, but just because I'm interested. You don't need to
do this, of course; it's easier and more helpful to keep a "price book"
with the cost of items you buy regularly. For example, your notebook
might look something like this:

Store	12 oz. orange juice		1 loaf whole-wheat bread		16 oz. frozen peas	
National	Name brand	1.69	Name brand	1.89	Name brand	1.89
	Store brand	1.39	Store brand	1.49	Store brand	1.49
	Generic	.99	Generic	.99	Generic, none	
A&P	Name brand	1.49	Name brand	1.99	Name brand	1.69
	Store brand	1.09	Store brand	1.29	Store brand, none	
	Generic	.89	Generic, none		Generic	1.59

On the first line of the chart, across from National, I have recorded
brand-name prices. Line two is store brand prices, and line three,
generic. To compile the information for your price book, you can do
all your shopping at National one week and quickly jot down prices as
you buy. Next week do the same at A&P, and so on until you've com-
pleted a list for three or more stores. The store with the overall low-
est prices could then be your base store.

Supermarkets are only one possibility. I have checked out—and
continue to check out—discount and wholesale grocers, food co-
ops, day-old bakeries, produce stands, farmers' markets, dairies, buying clubs, cheese factory outlets, meat markets, scratch-and-dent

outlets, and health food stores. In the past few years, I've been buying most of my spices from Olde Town Spice Shoppe, in a historic district near my home. We've even found cheap tomatoes, in season, at a florist's. You never know where you'll uncover a bargain.

To research possibilities, you might want to start with your telephone company's yellow pages under "Grocers" and/or "Food." Even if you live in a rural area, I think you'll be surprised at what you may find in your phone book. Also, talk to friends and neighbors about good buys in your area, wherever you live. I've gotten some great leads just by asking around.

3. *Buy most groceries from the cheapest store.*

This may seem so obvious it's hardly worth mentioning. It's surprising, though, how many people will only shop someplace that offers them spotlessly waxed floors and calculators on the carts. I understand. But such stores are usually not the places where you'll save the most money.

My personal favorite is Aldi, a no-frills discount warehouse that offers a limited selection of foods, but at about 50% below most supermarket prices. It's amazing how much cheaper some stores are than others. Many products at Aldi, for example, cost less than supermarket brand names advertising a half-price savings! In other words, when a local supermarket's "special" on wheat bran cereal is $1.69, Aldi's store brand price is $1.29 (with little, if any, difference in quality). This is why it is so important to price check by referring to your notebook, then select a base store that offers the best deals.

4. *Supplement by shopping at other stores whose weekly specials are outstanding, or use alternative strategies.*

Did you know that supermarkets sometimes take a loss on a few items in order to entice you to buy there? "Loss leader" specials, some or all of those advertised on the front and back of weekly flyers, may actually be priced below a store's cost. You can easily spot the real bargains by quickly leafing through several ads, price notebook in hand. It takes me about five minutes to decide on my second store for the week, based on the items that I need that are on sale. In another ten minutes, I've combed through that store's ad a second time and have my shopping list written.

I often stop at three or four food stores a week. This is not as difficult as it sounds, since three are within an eight-mile radius of my home. One of the children (my shopping assistant for the week) and I usually swing by the produce stand first. Next we often shop at IGA, then Aldi. By dedicating one afternoon a week to both food and supply shopping, plus other errands, we're able to get almost everything done in three to four hours total. Then, Michael stops by the Pepperidge Farm bread store every week or so after picking up Eric after work.

Over the last several years, I've begun to use several alternative strategies in addition to smart shopping. I do much more cooking and baking from scratch, for example, and we continue to try to garden. (You can read more on these strategies, and dozens of others, in the next two chapters.)

5. *Make a detailed shopping list.*

As I write down items I need for the week, I try to match up ideas for meals with store specials. If fish is on sale, for example, I buy and serve that instead of roast beef. Though my basic menus are planned well in advance, the overall structure is flexible so that I can take advantage of cheaper foods.

My shopping list starts with essentials, and then I add other food I would also like to buy. I estimate the total cost for everything on my list. If I'm under $84 I can add more; if over, I delete a few items and rethink my meal plans. Sometimes I take extra money with me, but most days I'm within a few dollars of my estimate.

Substitutions are justified when I find an unexpected good deal. Aldi sometimes has surprise specials, like "buy one, get one free" loaves of whole-wheat bread. When I find a bargain like this, I cross some long-term baking items off my list and stock up as much as I can.

But in order to demonstrate just how my system works, I want to begin by sharing an actual shopping list and menu plans for seven consecutive days. I recorded both the items I bought and how I used them throughout the following calendar week.

Below, I'll detail the first list and total prices, then explain why I bought what I did. You'll also find a record of my next two shopping lists and fourteen consecutive days of menus in the Appendix.

SHOPPING LIST, WEEK #1

Aldi

4 pounds white sugar	$1.35
2 pounds brown sugar	.89

12-ounce can evaporated milk	$ .49
18-ounce box cornflakes	.89
15-ounce box sweetened puffed cereal	1.69
16-ounce package gourmet crackers	.99
16-ounce package pretzels	.89
15-ounce package tortilla chips	.89
16-ounce package graham crackers	.99
9 ounces cashews	2.29
24-ounce jar spear pickles	.99
15-ounce can pink salmon	1.39
8 6-ounce cans tuna	3.12
26 ounces spaghetti sauce	.99
3.5-ounce package sliced pepperoni	.99
3 pounds long-grain rice	.79
10 pounds bananas	2.99
29-ounce can peaches	.79
25-ounce jar applesauce	.59
2 pounds carrots	.79
7-ounce can mushrooms	.49
2 15-ounce cans green beans	.58
15-ounce can peas	.29
15-ounce can chili beans	.29
1 gallon 2% milk	2.20
1 gallon skim milk	1.89
16 ounces grated cheddar cheese	2.49
2 pounds margarine	.98
3 dozen large eggs	1.47
10-count package flour tortillas	.69
4 2.5-ounce packages chicken lunch meat	1.16
3 pounds hot dogs	1.99
8-pack hot dog buns	.39
12-ounce apple juice concentrate	.69
12-ounce orange juice concentrate	.69
12-ounce grape juice concentrate	.69
20 ounces powdered lemonade	1.29
6 ice cream bars	1.99
2 8-ounce containers whipped topping	1.38

Total, with tax:	$48.35

Mid-Towne IGA

14-ounce package fat-free hot dogs	$3.75
1 pound boneless beef chuck steak	1.53
5.4 pounds boneless turkey breast	6.93
8-ounce container fat-free yogurt	.89
Total, with tax:	$13.67

Vaccaro & Sons Produce

1 gallon 2% milk	$2.07
6 apples	1.47
6 ears sweet corn	.99
4 tomatoes	.99
1 large watermelon	2.99
6 peaches	2.87
2 cantaloupes	3.00
Damaged Produce	$2.00
5 packages lettuce salad	
2 packages coleslaw	
8 pineapples	
Total, with tax:	$17.07

Pepperidge Farm Day-Old Bread Store

4 24-ounce loaves 100% whole-grain bread	
Total, with tax:	$5.53

Wal-Mart

Eric, my shopping assistant for this week, and I miscommunicated, and neither of us bought bran flakes cereal at Aldi. I dropped by Wal-Mart after taking Eric to work early one morning and bought:

2 18-ounce boxes bran flakes with raisins	
Total, with tax:	$4.51

Grand Total, Week #1:	*$89.13*

The unexpected Wal-Mart trip for cereal put me over the budget by about $5. I'll make up for it next week, though (see the Appendix).

As you can tell from reading my list, I buy a lot of ordinary food. Most groceries for this week came from Aldi, as usual. The produce stand is less than a mile farther down the road. I often shop at IGA because its meat is excellent and it's convenient.

Perhaps you notice that my shopping list does not include any non-food items, like aluminum foil, paper towels, or laundry detergent. I buy some of these items at Aldi and some from Family Dollar, a few doors down from Aldi. We try to make do with reusable goods whenever possible, buy secondhand items, and recycle everything we can.

One of the ways in which we keep our grocery bills low is to avoid buying special, high-priced foods that are low in fat. My thinking is that instead of using large quantities of the low-fat items, why not smaller quantities of the regular version? In other words, buy regular sour cream at Aldi and use a teaspoon on your baked potato instead of two tablespoons of low-fat sour cream. The fat content turns out to be almost the same, the food tastes better, and the cost is much less.

We have tried to convert to lower-fat snack foods, substituting crackers, for example, in place of potato chips. We usually serve animal crackers (3 grams of fat per serving), graham crackers (4 grams), pretzels (1.5 grams), or other low-fat alternatives. I also try to bake extra muffins and breads for dinner at night, so the next day I have "fillers" to offer for lunch.

I purchase one container of Dannon plain nonfat yogurt every couple of weeks, and use it as starter to make twelve cups of homemade yogurt. I eat a cup of homemade yogurt for lunch every day, and find it a good source of calcium as well as a health benefit.

And now, here are the menus for breakfast, lunch, dinner, and two daily snacks—*real-life* menus, remember—that followed from my shopping.

MENUS, WEEK #1

Monday

Breakfast: Choice of granola,* cornflakes, instant oatmeal, oatmeal pancakes,* and/or fresh fruit, milk; Eric usually

---

* Starred items can be found in the Recipe Index. Look them up; you'll be surprised at the low-fat content.

eats two bowls of bran flakes cereal and a cup of store-bought yogurt each morning

Lunch: Bowtie pasta with spaghetti sauce, whole-grain bread and butter, grapes

Dinner: Grilled hamburgers, fresh green beans and onions,* baked beans, fresh fruit salad,* cantaloupe slices, potato chips, toasted marshmallows

Tuesday

Breakfast: Choice of granola,* cornflakes or bran flakes, instant oatmeal, pancakes, and/or fresh fruit, milk

Lunch: Grilled cheese sandwiches on whole-grain bread, peanuts, and raisins

Dinner: Enchiladas,* corn on the cob, lettuce salad, fresh pineapple slices, ice cream bars

Wednesday

Breakfast: Honey puffs cereal, milk; Mary ate a lettuce salad.

Lunch: Nachos and cheese, choice of fruit (grapes, cantaloupe, bananas), graham crackers

Snack: The two boys ate almost half a watermelon.

Dinner: Potato puffs casserole, breadmaker bread, coleslaw,* banana salad (peach yogurt with sliced bananas)

Thursday

Breakfast: Choice of granola,* cornflakes, instant oatmeal, milk

Lunch: Leftover enchiladas,* corn chips, cantaloupe, pineapple

Dinner: Turkey breast (cooked in the Crock-Pot), baked potatoes, gravy, whole-grain bread (store bought) slices, canned peas, coleslaw,* tomatoes

Friday

Breakfast: Choice of granola,* cornflakes, instant oatmeal, fresh fruit, milk

Lunch: Chicken, bean, and noodle soup,* Goldfish crackers (from the day-old bread store), sliced apples, bananas

Dinner: Red beans and rice,* lettuce salad with low-fat French dressing,* pumpkin/zucchini bread,* pineapple-banana salad

Late-night snack: Hot dogs and potato chips; Dad took this out to our four campers in the backyard tent.

Saturday
Breakfast: Pumpkin/zucchini bread,* milk
Lunch: Peanut butter and jelly sandwiches on whole-grain bread, graham crackers, choice of fruit
Dinner: Homemade pizza,* breadsticks,* lettuce salad, sliced carrots, pineapple with whipped topping

Sunday
Breakfast: Choice of granola,* cornflakes, instant oatmeal, fresh fruit, milk
Lunch: Lunch out (we consider this part of our entertainment budget)
Dinner: Leftover red beans and rice,* leftover peanut butter sandwiches, cantaloupe, pretzels

Most days I'm very diligent about making sure we all get the proper vitamins and minerals needed. If anyone wants a snack, he or she is welcome to load up on an assortment of fresh fruits, home-made frozen juice ice pops, and/or carrot sticks. We serve one fruit, often two, with every lunch, and three vegetables and/or fruits with every dinner in addition to the optional fruit snacks. As mentioned earlier, all six of us take daily, high-quality food-form supplements.

Besides providing milk for drinking, I add generous portions of nonfat dry milk to my bread (and sometimes main dish) recipes. We often drink orange juice for dinner. We recently bought a cheap water purifier and try to drink eight glasses of water a day; to encourage drinking, there's always a pitcher of cold water in the refrigerator.

Sometimes I'm a bit lax in planning varied, interesting meals, and that's why there were two consecutive dinners featuring chicken breasts this week. You may also notice the repetition of pineapple dishes; I got a great deal on pineapples while shopping, and so we ate a lot while the fruit was still fresh and delicious.

I eat almost everything the children eat. Michael is on a restricted diet, and I buy certain foods, like fat-free hot dogs, exclusively for him. He also makes his own diet hot chocolate.

Most of the time, we go without nightly desserts. I'm a sugar junkie, so this has been quite a sacrifice, though a good one, for me.

Sometimes Mary, age ten, gets into a baking mood and we enjoy her sweet treats for a few meals. Then we try to get back on track.

As you can imagine, I cook fairly large quantities so there's prepared food available for future meals. Sometimes we share leftovers for lunch, sometimes I serve them "straight" or recycled at dinner, and sometimes I freeze whatever is left. I normally shop on Tuesdays, so on Mondays I use up as many leftovers as possible. The spaghetti sauce this week, for example, was actually cooked a few weeks earlier and frozen. Monday night's fruit salad contained a variety of odds and ends of fruit, and I still had a few baked beans left over from a weekend barbecue.

My meals do not always exactly reflect what was bought that week. For example, Monday dinner's main dish, grilled hamburgers, came from a frozen 10-pound package I purchased at Wal-Mart two weeks before. I try to buy food on a rotating basis so that each week when I go shopping, there's already a surplus available in my cupboard and freezer that allows more choices.

Remember, I promised real-life menus. It was very tempting to doctor these listings and show you perfectly balanced meals. Unfortunately, I don't always succeed in feeding us perfectly. At one point, I considered recording menus as I *planned* to serve them, a model for the month, so to speak. But I thought it might be more helpful to play "true confessions" and tell you what we really ate for three weeks.

I am not trying to justify my menus or suggest that you try to follow them. Not at all. These listings are here to give you an idea of exactly what I do and do not serve within the restraints of my self-imposed $12-a-day budget. I know you'll want to plan your own system, your own menus, and your own recipes to help your family eat healthy and inexpensively. Turn to the next chapter for some additional strategies to help save money on nutritious food.

CHAPTER 2

Beat the System at the Store

Several years ago I really didn't know much about saving money on food. Since then, I've discovered ways to circumvent the marketing strategy—that is, to "beat the supermarket system"—through careful buying of loss leader sale items and marked-down goods like meat and produce. I've also learned more about bulk buying at warehouse stores, large-scale couponing, refunding, and other smart shopping principles. Today, I get a lot more food for my money than I used to get.

As I mentioned in the last chapter, there are all sorts of retail and wholesale outlets where you can purchase low-cost groceries. The trick is to beat the system at that particular store.

SAVE MONEY ON WHAT YOU BUY

Let's assume that you've already chosen a base store and are ready to do some serious shopping. Before you even begin, beware of "supermarket [or warehouse store, etc.] seduction." You know what I mean: aisle upon aisle of luscious displays, a real temptation for your senses. Keep in mind that grocery stores ordinarily make only a narrow profit margin on most foods. Stores rake in the most money from overpriced convenience foods and nonfood goods like cosmetics and cleaners. There's nothing wrong with the supermarket's employing please-put-me-in-your-cart strategies, but there's also no reason why you have to buy into the seduction.

11

So take your list along and stick to it. Go to the store well rested, if you can. Buy generic, slightly damaged, marked-down, or store brand groceries whenever possible. Try to purchase large quantities in order to drop per-ounce costs. And above all, keep in mind why you're doing this: You have better things to do with the money you're *not* spending on food.

That said, here are some guidelines for saving money on specific foods when you shop in stores.

Meats

Watch carefully for sales and stock up on the feature of the week. Buy a month's worth of chicken at 59 cents a pound, and next week a month's worth of beef roast for half price. Some supermarkets feature family packs, with quantity meat offered at a discount.

When turkeys and hams go on sale during Thanksgiving and Christmas, try to have enough money set aside to invest in more than one for your freezer. Later, you can substitute turkey for chicken in all your chicken recipes.

Purchase whole chickens and cut them up yourself; all you need is a very sharp knife and a standard cookbook's directions. If you cut, skin, and bone your own chicken breasts, you'll probably spend about $1 a pound or less for these "gourmet pieces," the ones that ordinarily fetch $4 a pound and more. You can also bag and freeze like pieces—all wings, or legs, for example—for use in future meals.

Consider buying meat in quantity. You may be able to purchase half a side of beef at the meat market, or from a farmer, for a price 50% less than the supermarket's. Find a few friends with freezer space, and you're all set. Negotiate directly with the meat manager when you plan to buy large quantities of meat. Jill Bond, my friend who prepares six months' worth of meals at a time, often does so and saves considerably.

Buy fish or seafood that is currently in season.

Rely on cheaper brands of turkey or chicken cold cuts and hot dogs rather than those made from beef and pork.

Ask meat managers if they mark down overbuys. I once found a local store that sold surplus meat at half price or less. While you're asking, find out if there are discounts offered on the "ends" of deli meat loaves.

Cost compare, and you may be able to buy on-sale meat from a butcher for a competitive price. If so, ask him to give you the bones and other throwaways along with the prime cuts; you can make them into soups and broths.

Dairy Foods

Purchasing milk products at the supermarket can be expensive, but there are other options. You may have to shop around to find the best prices. Start with a membership warehouse club, Aldi, Super Wal-Mart, Save-A-Lot, or similar store. Can you locate a dairy or cheese outlet through your local yellow pages? Even driving some distance for milk products may be worth a once-a-month trip, especially if you buy in large quantities and freeze milk and cheese.

Buy "ends" of cheese rolls at the deli section; some supermarkets mark these down in price.

Sometimes grated cheese, sold by the pound at in-store salad bars, may be cheaper than cheese in the dairy section.

Many dairy foods—milk substitutes, soft margarine, low-fat sour cream, whipped topping, yogurt, and even yogurt cheese—can be made cheaply from scratch. See the Recipe Index under "Milk Substitutes and Products."

Name Brand Goods

If you're a loyal name brand buyer because you like the taste of the food, you may want to reconsider buying store brands instead. Here's why. Almost all store brands are manufactured by name brand companies; that is, two identical cans of green beans may be labeled as either name brand or store brand, depending only on when the factory's assembly line setup is changed. The can of store brand green beans at your local supermarket is probably a name brand can with a different label—and a much cheaper product at that.

A friend of mine once walked through a grocery store with two carts. In one cart, he placed name brand products at regular price. In the other cart, he placed exactly the same products, store brand versions, also at regular price. The difference between the two carts at the checkout was between 30% and 40%, a savings of, say, $3 to $4 for every $10 worth of food purchased, with virtually no extra effort. That's another good reason to buy store brands.

If a particular can of store brand peaches doesn't taste like those Del Monte peaches you love, it's probably because Del Monte makes a different store brand. Try another label to find one that matches the quality of your favorite name brand.

One mother of young children told me that, because of TV advertising, her children insisted on eating only name brand Cheerios. She consented, bought a box of Cheerios, emptied the contents into a plastic cereal container, and made sure the children saw the box on the counter. From that time on, she purchased the store brand equivalent of Cheerios and emptied it into the same cereal container, throwing away the box in secret. Her children never knew the difference.

Generic goods are another possibility, though the quality can be mixed: sometimes excellent, sometimes good, and sometimes inferior. I'd suggest you purchase one generic product every week and try it out. If you're unhappy with the product, every supermarket I know will gladly take the returned, partly used item and refund your money. Then you can mark that item off your price list permanently.

Produce

As a rule, don't buy fresh fruits and vegetables at the supermarket unless you can find them as "loss leaders" or discounted through a particularly good sale.

Ask the store's produce manager if he or she would be willing to set out bags of slightly brown bananas for half price. Find out what he or she does with damaged produce and volunteer to buy it at a discount.

Wherever you shop, purchase only what's in season and/or on sale. Apples, of course, are common in the fall, as are pumpkins and winter squash. Oranges and grapefruits peak in November through April. Strawberries are best in late spring. (See the chart "Peak Season for Fruits and Vegetables" on page 180.)

Weigh bagged produce to find the one that's slightly heavier. You may discover a two-pound bag, for example, that holds two and a half pounds of carrots.

Try to process older and damaged produce immediately for maximum nutrition and minimum waste. If leafy vegetables are wilted, pick off the brown edges, sprinkle with cool water, wrap in a towel, and refrigerate. You can freeze most fruits and vegetables in airtight containers, freezer bags, or recycled boxed cereal liners; to get most of the air out and prevent freezer burn, seal the top except for one tiny corner, insert a straw into the bag and suck out excess air, then quickly close. Consult a standard cookbook for more specific advice on what can and cannot be frozen.

Fresh produce is best for you, and the fresher the better. Canned fruits and vegetables have less nutritional value and a higher sodium content than frozen or fresh equivalents. But if you must rely on canned produce, look for store brand, generic, or on-sale name brands whenever possible. Those who cook in large quantities should consider buying institutional-size cans of vegetables, which are often much cheaper per ounce than their smaller counterparts. Another alternative is to purchase generic frozen vegetables, then steam them in a covered saucepan; the cost will probably be higher, but so will the vitamin content.

Breads and Grains

Compare prices carefully in your area to find the best low-cost source of breads. I used to buy from a day-old bakery, saving about 50% over supermarket prices. Then for several years I purchased Aldi brand wheat loaves, until I learned that there was little whole-wheat flour in the recipe. Now we buy 100% whole-grain bread from a Pepperidge Farm outlet store, $1.29 for one-and-a-half-pound loaves.

Bulk buy whole-grain products like oats and cornmeal; baking supplies like flour and yeast; as well as beans, brown rice, and pasta. Check the bulk buy section of your supermarket or . . .

BULK BUY FROM MEMBERSHIP WAREHOUSE CLUBS

Several years ago, Michael and I were given a free membership in a membership warehouse club, Sam's, just down the road. I checked out the store and found good prices and good quality. So we tried stocking up on, among other things, Cap'n Crunch cereal and tortilla chips.

It was fun while it lasted. The only trouble was, it didn't last as long as it was supposed to. For us, buying ten times our normal amount of chips didn't mean we had chips ten times as long. It meant we ate a lot more a lot faster. Our problem with buying in bulk is that we tended to eat in bulk, too.

It is not this way for everyone. I know of some families who visit the wholesale club, stock-up stores, and other outlets once a month, buy wisely, and then consume wisely. Stocking up on items like yeast, for example, makes sense; it stays tucked away in the refrigerator, and you can't sit down in front of the TV and overindulge in it.

Mike Yorkey, in his excellent book, *Saving Money Any Way You*

Can, interviewed an anonymous warehouse club insider for insight into how these clubs work. Most surprising to me was "Paul"'s explanation that his own company, Price Club[1], makes no money on merchandise, selling goods at cost. As Paul says, "If it weren't for the annual membership fees, we couldn't stay in business." Warehouse club merchandise is normally marked up about 10% higher than wholesale cost, rather than 25% for most discount chains' goods, and 50% for other retailers'.

Membership warehouse clubs eliminate middlemen—plus all of the expenses of both distributors and additional freight—by shipping goods directly from the manufacturer to their warehouses. They also save by minimizing the number of salespeople and eliminating fancy fixtures. Costs are cut to the bone in order to keep prices low. To make up for lost profits, membership warehouses charge fees to "qualified" individuals who want to shop their stores. Qualifications are so broadly defined that almost anyone can participate.

Prices are obviously good; what you have to determine, as a smart consumer, is this: Will I save enough money buying at the club this year to justify the cost of membership? In certain parts of the country, you probably will; in others, perhaps not.

When and if you shop at warehouse clubs, follow this advice:

- Look around on your first visit. Note prices, unit costs, and quantities before you buy.
- Make a list and stick to it. Don't allow yourself to linger and be tempted.
- Buy just enough to last until your next visit. In the meantime, you will probably be able to use other shopping strategies that might save you more money.
- Go at a time that's less hectic than rush hour.
- Don't buy products you can get cheaper elsewhere.
- Don't buy products just to try out at home. Make sure you really like and will use the product.
- Don't buy products that supposedly save you money if you're spending more in the long run by buying more (e.g., my tortilla chips story).
- Don't buy margarine, canned vegetables, meats, sodas, and bread at the warehouse, as you can usually find them at cost or below at supermarkets, especially with use of double coupons.

Paul, the anonymous Price Club employee, adds some insider tips: "Get to know some of the staff. They can tell you about the hot bargains or when something new is expected to arrive. They'll know which slow movers have been marked down, or when price changes are made."[2]

Paul also details Price Club's elaborate merchandise coding system; your local warehouse store probably uses a similar system, and personnel there could explain it to you. Ask about good buys. I did, and was referred to a damaged goods section at Sam's Club by a helpful clerk.

One more word on bulk buying from stores: Try to keep extra money set aside for the best bargains. Check stores regularly for damaged goods and loss leader items. Buy as much as you can afford when the price is right.

TRY THE PANTRY PRINCIPLE

Barbara Salsbury, a nationally recognized consumer specialist, sent me her video called *Beating the High Cost of Eating*. I was impressed with Barbara's research. She tells, for example, the inside story of how supermarkets excel at "super-marketing," doing all they can to convince you to buy plenty of food you really don't need at premium prices.

One of the most interesting concepts Barbara shares is the Pantry Principle, her strategy for keeping the pantry continually well stocked through careful buying. Here's how it works, in Barbara's own words.

The habit of stocking up on items when the price is right yields constant savings. Even if you have to put off buying a few nonessential items . . . use the money you would have spent on them to establish the routine of stocking up when those prices are right. For example: If you know you use canned pineapple about twice a month, plan to buy a case or half case when the case lot sales are scheduled. You won't need to buy pineapple again for several weeks or perhaps several months, or until you see it at a price you are willing to pay. Next shopping trip your list will not have to include these "stocked-up" items—which in turn gives you more buying power to follow the same strategy again. The bargains, benefits, and buying power will begin to compound! Taking into account your space, budget, and storage life of the items on sale, stock up on groceries and other items you consistently use when they are at rock-bottom prices. If you are shrewd you can start buying items only when they are at the best prices and never pay full price for them again.[3]

Stocking up on good buys is not a new concept, of course, but Barbara has this principle down to a science. Using the Pantry Principle is certainly one valid way to save money on food.

USE COUPONS

Maybe you're looking for additional ways to save money at the supermarket. If so, large-scale couponing and/or refunding may be the answer for you.

Some time ago, *Cheapskate Monthly* newsletter featured a woman who claimed to have saved a total of $17,433.17 over the course of about fifteen years *solely* through the use of coupons and refunds. Twice a week, Mary Ann Maring spent at least an hour scanning the ads for local supermarkets, clipping store coupons and determining the best buys for what she needed. Next she went through her extensive files, matching up manufacturers' coupons with sales and store coupons wherever possible. To keep current, Mary Ann purged her files every four months. Expired coupons were pitched, and soon-to-expire ones were rotated to the front of each category.

Mary Ann's approach was intriguing: She learned to play the couponing game to great personal advantage. As *Cheapskate Monthly* noted, "There were many items for which she would pay only a few cents and occasionally she pointed out an item she would be getting absolutely free."

Once in a while I do use coupons. Recently at the supermarket I picked up two candy bars for five cents each, five cans of name brand vegetables for 60 cents total, and two bottles of Softsoap for 60 cents each. I know couponing works. But I must admit I don't think, generally speaking, it merits a significant investment of my time.

For example, by using coupons, the Del Monte vegetables cost 15 cents a can. The same size private label corn is 29 cents a can at my base store, Aldi. I honestly can't detect a difference in taste. And to save 14 cents a can, I had to find a store featuring Del Monte vegetables on sale, clip a coupon, search the shelves a few moments to find an exact match, and redeem a double coupon. Maybe I dislike all of this bother because I place a high premium on the value of my time. I want things quick and easy, and the extra work for fourteen pennies is simply not worth it to me.

And here's another problem. Most coupons are printed for highly packaged convenience foods, like expensive ready-to-eat cereal or salad dressings. So even if I buy on sale with double coupons, I may still pay more for an item that I can make myself.

A while back at the grocery store, I did a cost comparison of three items at original price and after double coupons, contrasting with both a name brand and Aldi's brand. Here's what I discovered:

Lucky Charms cereal cost $3.69; with a 50 cent coupon doubled, $2.69. But I could buy a similar product, same size, at Aldi for $1.69. Or I could serve my entire family home-cooked oatmeal for breakfast for less than 50 cents, or eggs and toast for about $1.

Yoplait yogurt cost 69 cents; with a "30 cents off 2" coupon doubled, 39 cents each. At Aldi, yogurt was 29 cents for the same size; and homemade, at about 15 cents, is even cheaper.

Log Cabin Syrup cost $3.29; with a 40 cent coupon doubled, $2.49. Aldi's version was 89 cents for a smaller size, or $1.78 for two equaling the Log Cabin bottle; and homemade cost 50 cents or less.

If saving money is your main goal, you would have to locate these items on sale and double a coupon to even approach the cost of the homemade products. This is possible, especially when making use of what serious couponers call single, double, and triple plays; and grand slams. Mike Yorkey describes how it works:

> The simplest transaction is a "single play," which takes place when a consumer uses a standard cents-off coupon, such as a straight 50 cents off a box of Rice Krispies. But you can do more. . . . Let's say your local supermarket is having a buy-one, get-one-free sale on Ragu spaghetti sauce. The cost of each jar is $1.77. You pull two jars of Ragu off the shelf and take two Ragu coupons out of your file box. If you have two coupons for 50 cents off, that's a "double play." Final cost: 77 cents.
>
> But if you're shopping in a supermarket that doubles coupons, you can go for a "triple play"! Again, you pull two jars of Ragu off the shelf for $1.77. Then, you take two Ragu coupons out of your file box. Each doubled 50-cent coupon is

worth $1, for a total of $2. Because you paid $1.77 for the two jars but received $2 at the checkout stand, the supermarket just paid you 23 cents to purchase two jars of Ragu. . . .

The ultimate coupon play is a "grand slam." That's when you have manufacturers' coupons and store coupons (found in newspaper inserts) in your file box. Let's say the store is again offering the two-for-one deal on Ragu sauce. In your hot little hands, you're holding two 50-cent manufacturers' coupons, which when doubled equal $2 off. But the supermarket also has in-store coupons for 25 cents off, which double to 50 cents each for a total of $1. In all, you receive a $3 refund, which means the grocer just paid you $1.23 to put two jars of Ragu into your cart.[4]

Believe it or not, this is legal. And though the work involved may be mind-boggling, there is a certain thrill in achieving a "grand slam."

Couponing may be a viable option for you if you think of it as a hobby, enjoy name brand products, or have a difficult time finding discounted food. Here are some recommendations for novices from Jackie Iglehart, of *The Penny Pincher* newsletter, and Mary Kenyon, an expert couponer:

- To find coupons, subscribe to the Sunday newspaper, or check the food section of the daily paper, women's magazines, and boxes at the front of some supermarkets.
- Ask willing friends and relatives to save coupons for you. Consider setting up a coupon exchange box at the library.
- Look over couponing magazines (see Resources under "News-letters") to decide whether a subscription is worth your while.
- Clip all coupons and file them in appropriate categories, such as "Breads," "Meats," and "Frozen Foods."
- Make a coupon file from a small box, tabbed and divided by cardboard pieces. Always take your coupon box along when you leave home.
- Decide ahead of time what coupons you will use at the store, and transfer them to an envelope. Arrange the coupons in the order that you find foods placed in store aisles, on your usual route, or alphabetically.
- Don't buy an item just because you have a coupon unless it's something you'd use anyway, or unless it's free or nearly free.

- Besides buying on sale, try to use coupons for products that you find in damaged or discontinued bins.
- Stockpile when you find a particularly good deal.
- Take advantage of rain checks. If a store is out of a sale product for which you have coupons, ask Customer Service to give you a "voucher" that can be redeemed at a later time.

Cheapskate Monthly suggests you may be an excellent candidate for couponing if you like to organize things, have tenacity and patience, can see the big picture, are flexible, and enjoy a challenge.

But if you're thinking, as I am, that this is just too much work, then large-scale couponing may not be for you. Says Amy Dacyczyn, author of *The Tightwad Gazette*, "I feel that using couponing and refunding as your major grocery strategy will reduce your food bill, but not as much as if you use a combination of strategies." In the end, it comes down to personal preference.

DO REFUNDING

Some of us have taken advantage of a refund offer or two. Perhaps we've dutifully clipped the UPC symbol from a box of cereal, mailed it in, and received a check for $1 in the mail. I never found myself too enthusiastic about a return of a couple of bucks a month, especially considering the work and postage involved. Then again, there are ways to use refunding as a major means of saving money on groceries.

The Tightwad Gazette newsletter once described Mary Kenyon of Independence, Iowa, who (several years ago) spent about $385 monthly to feed a family of six. What's remarkable about it? Well, Mary saved an average of 20% of that amount through coupon use, and received back $110 each month on refunds, even after postage. That brought her weekly grocery bill down to $50.

I gave Mary a call to learn more. She told me that, at the time, she was saving almost 30% off the cost of food through couponing. But what I really wanted to know about was refunding: Exactly how does one get back all that money? Mary wrote:

"I save all my labels, receipts, and UPC symbols and file them in Ziploc bags according to product categories (i.e., juice, aspirin, cereal, crackers). I have two file cabinets and shelves with boxes to hold my qualifiers. I have several traders (other refunders) who I regularly trade refund forms and complete deals with. This way I am able to take advantage of many more refunds that are put out by manufacturers each month. . . . I spend 15–20 hours a week working on refunding, in 15-minute to half-hour stretches. This includes clipping and sorting coupons, planning a grocery list, cutting and filing qualifiers, sending out for refunds, and organizing trades."

What does all this effort get Mary? "I provide 85% of my children's Christmas gifts through my refunding," she explained. "I usually have extra T-shirts and watches to give to my brothers and have also given baskets of trial-size products and food products I've gotten free with coupons to my mother, a sister, or an elderly shut-in." In addition, "After postage ($15 to $20 a month), I average $90 in cash, another $25 to $35 in free product coupons, and five to twenty free gifts back. If you subtract that $90 in cash from what I spent on groceries, then I really did save a great deal."

Michele Easter, onetime publisher of *Refunding Makes Cents!* (*RMC*), says, "I receive many checks in the mail every month by taking the time to peel labels, cut off UPCs, and mail away for cash, gifts, and free coupons. I mail for at least 100 refunds every month on all types of household products. So my mailbox is stuffed with checks for $1, $5, $10, and more, and I receive free T-shirts, toys, tapes, etc., plus wonderful coupons for free full-size products."

I scanned the pages of an issue of *RMC*, and was impressed with both the scope and complexity of the bulletin. But I must confess I still have my doubts about refunding. For example, here is a typical offer:

"Ten free jars of Gerber 1st, 2nd, or 3rd Foods Baby Foods. Send 48 UPCs from Gerber baby foods or juices." Forty-eight jars of baby food, at an average price of 50 cents each, adds up to $24. You get ten free jars and so supposedly save $5. It all sounds impressive until you consider that forty-eight meals of a homemade equivalent, whipped up in the blender from your own delicious food, would only cost a few dollars or less. Which makes more sense, to *not* spend much money in the first place, or to spend a fair amount, then work at least an hour to get some of it back? Refunders claim big savings, but for my family, most of the time, it doesn't make cents *or* sense.

Here's another offer listed in *RMC*:

"Free mermaid doll. Send five UPCs from Chicken of the Sea products for a free doll. . . ." Oh yes, and there is a $1.95 postage and handling fee. So I buy five cans of name brand tuna at 89 cents each (the cheapest Chicken of the Sea product I could find), add p&h and arrive at a figure of $6.40 needed for my "free" doll. Wouldn't it be simpler, and much cheaper, to buy generic tuna at 49 cents a can? And pick up a mermaid doll—as we did—at a garage sale for a quarter? My total cost for five cans of tuna and a doll is $2.70. Who's really saving money here, not to mention time?

Refunders will argue that it's not that simple, and their lengthy newsletters bear witness to that. One way to make money through refunding, for example, is to trade forms that you already have to someone who doesn't have them. Over the past few years, there has been some controversy concerning newsletters' trading practices. Here's why: Serious refunders (and couponers) keep very organized files, containing store receipts and proofs-of-purchase from every product they buy. Most offers are limited to one per household. But it's very possible that one person will have on hand some surplus offers he or she can't use. Through newsletter ads, refunders can sell or trade these "complete deals" or forms.

Unfortunately, the manufacturers of coupon and refund forms take a dim view of trading. According to an article in *The Tightwad Gazette* newsletter, refunding newsletter publisher Ellen Biles of Georgia received twenty-one months in prison on four counts of mail fraud: Ellen submitted multiple refunds for the same offer and sold "complete deals" through the mail to an undercover postal inspector.[5] Amy Dacyczyn advises refunders to play it safe, submitting refunds only for products they bought, sending in exact purchase receipts, and reading the fine print carefully. Mary Kenyon agrees, adding that it's important to use only one address, one offer per family (if specified on the form), and legitimate cash register receipts for refund requests.

With all this in mind, refunding can be an enjoyable hobby that saves money on food. You'll find refund forms in the same places as coupons, and also on bulletin boards in stores, at courtesy desks, on specially marked packages, and even at cashiers' counters. To learn more about refunding, refer to the publications listed in Resources under "Newsletters."

CHECK OUT ALTERNATIVE STORES

You don't have to buy all your food at supermarkets or warehouse stores. There are often other kinds of retail establishments, some a little off the beaten path.

Produce Stands

I'm a regular customer at the stand of Vaccaro & Sons Produce. Dale, the manager, and I often say hello. I started asking a few years ago about the possibility of buying damaged produce and was told they had nothing available to sell. Through several conversations, I learned that a charity picked up damaged goods three mornings a week. On other days, especially hot summer days, less-than-perfect fruits and vegetables were thrown away. I changed my shopping day to Tuesday, when the damaged produce was available, and Dale and I worked out an agreement that I could buy it (when available) for $2 a box.

I hestitate to include this information because I think it's very important that customers buy from a store over a period of time, *paying full retail price and developing a relationship with an owner or manager*, before they ask for favors. Stores are concerned with the very real possibility that unethical customers will purposely damage goods in order to get a discount.

On the other hand, it seems a shame to me that good food goes to waste. Produce stands cannot sell even slightly damaged fruits and vegetables for full price. Think about it: If you have a choice, will you pick the apple with a small bruise or the perfect one? What happens to the bruised one? Once you find a produce stand with excellent prices, frequent it regularly, and gain the trust of the person in charge, you can ask about such damaged produce. The idea is to offer the owner or manager a mutually beneficial agreement: he or she makes a little money and you haul off what would otherwise be thrown away.

Keep your eyes open and you should be able to locate a seasonal produce stand in your area, or possibly even one that stays open year-round.

Pick-Your-Own Places

Pick-your-own places can provide not only a low-cost family outing but also a means of saving money on the freshest produce available. As the season—whether on strawberries, peaches, apples, or green beans—draws to an end, call occasionally and ask about the possibility of picking overripe fruit at a discount. A strawberry farm in Kirksville, Missouri, where we used to live, offered almost-free fruit to pickers at the end of the season.

If you know any farmers, friends of farmers, or relatives of farmers, ask about the possibility of helping to harvest a crop in exchange for a portion of it. Sometimes orchard owners, for example, have more fruit than they can handle, and welcome help.

Farmers' Markets

Farmers' markets abound in both big cities and rural areas. Be se lective and compare prices; some markets' prices are just as high as the supermarkets'.

Go late in the selling day, and preferably on the last selling day of the week, and you'll increase your chances of a spectacular buy. Farmers with excess produce usually want to unload their goods rather than haul them home again. You may be able to purchase boxes full of fruits and vegetables for practically nothing; friends of mine have done so.

Dairies

Sometimes a cheese factory or major dairy supplier owns an outlet store where cheese and other milk products are sold directly to the public at a discount. Check the yellow pages of your phone book under "Dairies."

If you live near a major university, call the general number to learn if the agricultural division of the university produces cheese and, if so, sells it.

Scratch-and-Dent Stores

A few people have told me there are stores that offer cans and other merchandise, slightly damaged, at huge discounts. Check the yellow pages under "Food" to learn if such a store is open in your area.

Health Food Stores

Surprisingly, health food stores can offer great deals on certain foods like bulk spices, whole grains, and nuts. I buy unsalted almonds at Nutrition Stop for about half the price of the supermarket's almonds.

Bakery Outlets (Day-Old Bread Stores)

Sometimes bakery outlets offer outstanding buys on breads, buns, cakes, crackers, and more. Shop around, as these stores' prices can vary widely. Our family loves the 100% whole-grain bread we buy at the Pepperidge Farm outlet store, a bargain at $1.29 for a one-and-a-half-pound loaf. Another outlet nearby, however, sells a one-pound loaf of all-white bread for 99 cents, *not* a good deal nutritionally or otherwise.

Get to know store personnel and find out the best times to buy merchandise. On some days of the week, for example, there will tend to be more overstock (and thus more selection and better prices) than on other days.

There you have it, several ways to beat the system at the store. And did you know there are other strategies you can use to cut your grocery bill, even without setting foot in a supermarket? Chapter 3 shows you how.

NOTES

1. Price Club at one time merged with Costco to form PriceCostco, and now the club is called simply Costco. See listing of "Membership Warehouse Clubs" in Resources.

2. Much of this information came from *Saving Money Any Way You Can,* © 1994, by Mike Yorkey. Published by Servant Publications, Box 8617, Ann Arbor, MI 48107. Direct quotes, from page 59 of *Saving Money,* are used with permission. See Resources, "Books and Booklets."

3. From the January, 1989 issue of *The Shopper's Report,* a monthly newsletter by Barbara Salsbury. Published by Salsbury Enterprises, 9198 Tortellini Drive, Sandy, UT 84093. Used with permission. See Resources, "Miscellaneous Products."

4. From *Saving Money Any Way You Can,* pages 43–44, 1994, by Mike Yorkey. Published by Servant Publications, Box 8617, Ann Arbor, MI 48107. Used with permission. See Resources, "Books and Booklets."

5. This information, from *The Tightwad Gazette* newsletter, is now included in *The Tightwad Gazette* books. See Resources, "Books and Booklets."

CHAPTER 3

Other Ways to Beat the System

One of the frustrating aspects of writing this book is that just when I think I've covered it all, new information comes in. Consider these ways to save on food: belonging to a co-op, bartering, organizing better for better savings, meal planning, cooking once a month, Megacooking, making or cooking more of your own food, gardening, preserving your food, gleaning, using government programs (as a last resort), and eating sensibly. What a list of strategies! If you don't enjoy shopping at grocery stores—or can't save as much as you'd like to there—then several other cost-cutting options are available to you.

BELONG TO A COOPERATIVE

I used to think of co-ops as groups of outdated hippie-type people who dined on unpalatable organic food. Ridiculous, I know, but I confess this stereotype lingered in the back of my mind until just a few years ago.

When I began to seriously investigate cooperatives, it was a pleasant surprise to meet ordinary folks who were enthusiastic about their work. The National Cooperative Business Association (NCBA), for example, offers a free listing of helpful publications you can buy to learn more about co-ops. I called NCBA and requested its no-cost, how-to-get-started packet, finding it very informative.

What advantages are there in joining a food-buying co-op? Members are attracted for a number of reasons, some as simple as socializing with like-minded neighbors, some as noble as helping our environment by eliminating much of the packaging used in supermarket foods.

Another important drawing point is big savings—at least over health food store prices—on organic foods. I consulted a catalog from Blooming Prairie Warehouse in Iowa City, Iowa, supplier for nearly a dozen co-ops in the St. Louis area. Selection is large and varied. Local co-op contact person Laurie Lowe explained, "Many members are concerned not only with cost, but also in buying quality organic and natural products." Laurie particularly likes the delicious cheese she purchases through Blooming Prairie.

Just what is a cooperative, and how does one operate? By definition, a co-op is simply a group of people who pool their resources to buy food in wholesale quantities at wholesale prices. Members consolidate several individual orders into a single group order, collect payment, and place the order with a wholesaler. When the food arrives, members unload it from the delivery truck and break it down into individual orders again. This process is usually repeated every few weeks.

Most wholesalers do require a minimum order of at least $500, but several families buying together can add up dollars quickly. The more you order, the more you save, so to speak.

A majority of co-op members are involved with one of the huge warehouses, like Blooming Prairie. But options vary widely. Jill Bond, author of *Mega-Cooking*, says individuals may be able to work with wholesalers directly: in other words, if you pre-prepare food in large quantities and place one $500 order once a year, you don't need to "cooperate" with anybody else. And of course, you can organize a very informal—or very small—co-op. Not long ago, I met a woman whose circle of friends took turns buying produce from Produce Row, a kind of farmers' market for wholesalers, here in St. Louis. Every week, one of the five families collected everyone's money and bought ultrafresh fruits and vegetables in quantity, at wholesale prices, then delivered one fifth of the goods to each family.

There are advantages to these smaller, informal co-ops, like more flexibility and greater control over getting exactly what you want. But connecting with a warehouse does offer tremendous choice. Blooming Prairie's 150-page, fine-print catalog goes into great detail; it even tells you if any given food is fruit juice–sweetened; has salt, wheat, or yeast in it; and meets organic standards. Members are also assured that they will receive plenty of help, including access to technical and computer support, a lending library, meetings and seminars, a newsletter, and more.

Joining any kind of food-buying co-op requires involvement. Depending on the organization, you may be asked to help recruit members, plan meetings, order, do paperwork, bag, divide into individual orders, and more. Some storefront co-ops request that their members wait on customers in the store. And others will allow you to forgo all the work if you're willing to pay more.

Finding the time to help may be a problem. Because many families these days have very few spare hours, some cooperatives have tried to introduce a new type of buying club, one in which a coordinator is paid a percentage of the club's sales in return for doing all the work. You organize and run the co-op, you get the price breaks and a commission. This may be an option for some.

As with any kind of food buying, self-restraint is a must. Take convenience foods, for example: co-ops offer them, just as the supermarket does. In one of Blooming Prairie's catalogs, I found items as diverse as Raviolini with Vermont Cheddar and Walnuts, Jumbo Oat Bran Fruit Bars, and Jammin' Corn and Potato Chowder. Whatever its form, recipe, or brand name, a convenience food is still more expensive than making it yourself. Those who buy through a co-op must be just as shrewd in their purchases as those who buy at stores.

Does belonging to a co-op really save you money? That depends. Is it important to you to purchase organic raisins? Are you allergic to milk, and presently buying soy substitutes at a health food store? Do you use only olive oil—rather than generic vegetable oil—in your cooking? Then a co-op may be a cost-saving option.

On the other hand, if your eating habits are more meat-potatoes-and-apple-pie (I hope you're eating the healthier versions), you'll need to take a close look at what co-ops sell and how that relates to what you buy. Compare prices carefully; you may be able to acquire quality, healthy food more cheaply at local stores and outlets. Also remember that some, though not all, local organizations charge membership fees. Once informed, you'll be able to make an intelligent decision about whether or not cooperatives might save you money on your weekly grocery bill.

I have to admit that researching co-ops has made me reconsider joining one myself. Blooming Prairie's catalog contains especially good prices on some items I regularly use, like yeast and spices. It also offers "deep discount deals" each month. Buying in case stack volume may yield discounts ranging from 10% to 30%. You can even order a sample package of several foods (usually new industry products) to try for a low price. And then there's that good cheese I keep hearing about. . . .

If you're interested, refer to Resources, "U.S. Cooperative Food Warehouses," to locate a co-op in your area. Maybe I'll see you at the next meeting.

BARTER

Years ago, when I taught piano lessons, I bartered a semester's worth of lessons for several pounds of prime Wisconsin cheese. My student's father owned a cheese factory, so it was a real bargain for her and a lot of delicious free food for me.

One-on-one bartering is not uncommon. But now there's a new, more complicated twist: trade networks that help businesses work with each other on a noncash basis. Although rules vary among these networks, the principle is basically the same: several businesses band together in a trade exchange that lists their services or products to other members. When Company A "sells" $1,000 worth of services to Company B, then Company A receives $1,000 worth of trade dollars. Those trade dollars, in turn, can be used to "buy" goods or services from other businesses in the exchange.

National Commercial Exchange (N.C.E.)

Our former neighbors, specialists in chimney repair, told me about National Commercial Exchange. The Bufords had just joined N.C.E. Already they had cashed in some trade credits earned through their work for $700 worth of pediatric dental work, plus eyeglasses valued at $223. Because they are members of an exchange, the Bufords did not have to trade dollar for dollar with one individual. They could have bartered their earned trade credits with a restaurant, a caterer, or even a cheesecake company. (I'll bet you were wondering how I was going to relate all this to food.)

I called N.C.E. and learned that the local chapter is part of a national network. The St. Louis Association currently lists no supermarkets, but had at one time included some. N.C.E. or other bartering exchanges in your area may offer that option. By joining, you might be able to trade some of your personal goods and services for fruit baskets, wedding cakes, a catered dinner party, an evening out at a fine restaurant, or just plain groceries.

When a business joins National Commercial Exchange, it is billed a one-time membership fee (which can vary from $50 to a few hundred dollars), half of which can be paid in barter. In addition, the purchaser pays a 12% cash commission to the office each time a product or service is received. Sellers call N.C.E. for an authorization number and the buyer's account is credited. Receipts are kept by all parties, including the office. Members receive a detailed monthly statement recapping all purchases. There are also renewal fees yearly; each exchange has a different format.

In addition to record keeping, exchange organizations actively promote participating businesses in a number of ways. N.C.E. in St. Louis mails a monthly newsletter that includes advertising and lists of what members want. If a needed service or business is not already part of N.C.E., the association tries to enlist one.

SHARE

Joining a trade organization may or may not qualify as an important means of saving money on food. But there is another option: SHARE (Self-Help and Resource Exchange), headquartered in San Diego, California. SHARE is a nonprofit, national program whose primary goal is "to build community by helping people work together to stretch their food budget."

Here's how it works. A community organization—a church, tenants' group, or club, for example—fills out an application to become a host organization. This host provides a place where members and people in the neighborhood can register for discounted food packages. Each package is the same within each region, a $25 to $30 value for approximately $14. The standard version usually includes six to ten pounds of meat; four to seven fresh vegetables; two to four fresh fruits; pasta, rice, or cereal; and a few specialty items. Other kinds of packages are also available in some areas.

At registration, participants pledge two hours of community service for every package to be purchased. Pledges can be fulfilled through normal church and volunteer activities, or even through helping to package bulk foods at the SHARE warehouse. The host organization tallies the number of packages requested, places an order with local SHARE headquarters, and sends a team of volunteers to pick up and bring back the food.

SHARE doesn't quite fit into a "bartering" or "cooperative" category. The program is open to everyone who is commited to consistent community participation, so in a sense, a discounted food package is bartered for volunteer work. SHARE's volume-buying power gives it some of the advantages of—though little similarity to—a cooperative.

SHARE is rapidly expanding and may be in your area now or in the near future. To find a nearby location, see Resources under "Organizations and More."

GET ORGANIZED

Have you ever stood in your kitchen at 4:45 P.M., dismally scanning the shelves for ideas for dinner? That's me sometimes, hoping for miracle food that assembles itself fast and easily on the table. It doesn't happen. No need to panic; there are alternatives to chaos.

Meal Plan

We all know how to meal plan, right? We take out a calendar, jot down dinner menus for each day of the month, and we're all set to have picture-perfect suppers. At least that's the idea, and it's a good one. By planning ahead, we usually assure our families of better-quality, good-tasting, healthy food and adequate nutrition.

If you're looking for inspirational meal plans, I suggest a browse through your library's cookbook section; almost every cookbook has dozens of helpful ideas. When designing your menus, here are some general principles to keep in mind.

1. Make sure to allow space for leftovers. If you've already "booked" every day for October, and nobody's having last night's soup for lunch, you might want to leave a night free now and then for all the odds-and-ends eating.
2. Don't feel guilty if you fail to have gourmet dinners on the table every day. We sometimes have better things to do with our time than cook.
3. Plan variety, but also keep in mind what your family likes. I recently read a cookbook that said something like, "There's no excuse for fixing the same meal more than once every six months." That may be true for the adventuresome, but I don't

think I could sell the idea to my children. If they had their way, we'd have pizza 365 days a year.

4. Stay flexible. A meal plan can be expensive if you follow it rigidly, passing up discounted and cheaper foods at the supermarket for the sake of "staying with the program." If fryers are on sale for 39 cents a pound, forget the round steak dinner this Wednesday and serve oven-baked chicken instead.

Do Once-a-Month Cooking

If you're really serious about meal planning, Mimi Wilson and Mary Beth Lagerborg may have the answer. These women have written a comprehensive book called *Once-a-Month Cooking (A Time-Saving, Budget-Stretching Plan to Prepare Delicious Meals)*. Mimi and Mary Beth not only cook thirty entrees all at once, they also do the majority of their monthly grocery shopping on one day.

They explain, "Each entree is partially prepared or cooked and assembled in advance. Then they're put into sealed containers and stored in the freezer. When you're ready to serve a certain meal, all you have to do is thaw it, combine the ingredients, and cook the entree. And all that time-consuming preparation and cleanup are done at one time."[1]

To help even more, Mimi and Mary Beth provide detailed shopping lists and menu plans. By using their system, they promise several benefits: " . . . after we've prepared a month or two weeks of meals, we don't have to fall back on less-nutritious, quick-fix foods or the more costly restaurant meals. . . . You can also save more money—and lots of time—when you make fewer trips to the store. Once you have your entrees in the freezer, you've done a major portion of your food preparation for the month."[2] If you're cooking once every thirty days using Mimi and Mary Beth's system, you will have thirty different meals prepared and in the freezer by the end of one long cooking day.

The disadvantages I can see to once-a-month cooking are three-fold: (1) coming up with a substantial amount of cash, initially, to buy everything required for a month's worth of meals; (2) the difficulty of shopping for ingredients for specific meals with no flexibility built into the menu plans; and (3) exhaustion from spending an entire day cooking. Still, the system is worth considering, especially if it's adapted to accommodate cheaper, healthy foods. Many busy women I know swear by it.

Mega-Cook

If you're really, really serious about meal planning, take once-a-month cooking a step further, to Mega-cooking. Jill Bond, author of *Mega-Cooking*, prepares *six months'* worth of entrees at one time. Jill; her husband, Alan; and some of their four children work together as they cook huge batches of chili, lentil soup, sweet-and-sour meatballs, and thirty to forty other kinds of dishes, all divided into dinner-sized servings and frozen for later use. This system differs from once-a-month cooking in that many batches of the same dish are all prepared at one time.

Jill's system of Mega-cooking encourages the use of the reader's favorite recipes. You can cook as expensively or as economically as you like. There's also a tremendous cash advantage to buying in such large quantities. A Mega-shopper can purchase the biggest (and cheapest) sizes of canned goods, crates of fresh low-cost produce from the farmers' market, and discounted meat from a butcher who may sell 20-pound packages at near-wholesale prices. From a survey the Bonds conducted of people using their program, they found families averaging a yearly savings of $1,640 over what they were spending on groceries the year before.

How does Mega-cooking work? The organization required is, as you'd expect, thorough. Jill's family usually devotes a three-day weekend to preparing about 180 meals. To help others streamline their own system, *Mega-Cooking* provides plenty of good advice. Jill also offers workshops nationwide to help would-be Mega-cooks get started.

I know what you're thinking: who in the world would want to spend so much time preparing so much food? *Mega-Cooking* assures us that cooks actually save dozens, perhaps hundreds, of hours in the long run. For example, if I average one hour a night doing cooking and cleanup for 180 dinner meals, I've invested 180 hours (although I still have to wash the plates and silverware, of course; the Bonds do, too). Jill, Alan, and their children get the same job done in less than twenty hours, or about fifty hours of combined work. They save even more time by avoiding frequent trips to the supermarket. The result: a lot of free hours.

Mega-cooking can start small, of course, even something as simple as doubling tonight's lasagna recipe, then freezing the second portion. More ambitious Mega-cooks should be prepared to fall in a heap at the end of a day of intense food preparation. Also, like once-a-month cooking, Mega-cooking is expensive when one first pur-chases all the food needed for a few dozen—or almost two hun-dred—meals.

For others, though, Mega-cooking is appealing. Apart from saving both time and money, there's something to be said for having a freezer full of "pre-prepared" food on hand.

Use Leftovers

Menu planning is one part of good organization. Another, equally important, is wise use of leftovers. Rule #1 is to keep a tight inven-tory, either mental or written, of foods on hand in the freezer, cup-board, and refrigerator. Here are some ideas for using leftovers.

- Breads of all kinds: Freeze until you have a bag full. Make stuff-ing, garlic breadsticks, bread pudding, bread crumbs, or crou-tons.
- Fruits: Use in Jell-O, ice pops, or Frozen Fruit Delight (see Recipes). Ripe bananas add flavor to banana bread or cookies.
- Leftover turkey: Make soup, pot pie, or enchiladas. Substitute it for chicken in chicken dishes.
- Vegetables: Chop or puree and add to ground meat dishes, or store in a freezer "soup pot," ready to simmer when you have a pot's worth.
- A variety of leftovers: Serve for lunches or snacks. Or make a buf-fet night when you serve dabs of this and that along with a special dessert.

Most of the above ideas are mine. I must admit I was pretty proud of my expertise in thinking of them until I discovered *The Use-It-Up Cookbook (A Guide for Minimizing Food Waste),* by Lois Carlson Willand. Included in Lois's book are 190 pages of recipes and good advice, a reheating time chart, a storage guide for perishable foods, and much more. Name just about any food you can think of, and you can find it here, along with dozens of ways to creatively recycle it. See Resources.

Try the 24-Hour-in-Advance Meal Plan

Amy Dacyczyn, author of *The Tightwad Gazette* books, suggests a system of organizing meals that involves minimum advance planning.

Amy and her husband, Jim, scout out the best deals on food, then inventory their home supplies before buying. Most of their shopping is a once-a-month outing. But they don't hesitate to make a special side trip, when running errands, to stores with particularly good deals. They also stock up on large quantities of food that go on sale less often.

Actual meal planning occurs the night before, 24 hours in advance. Either Jim or Amy decides what to serve for dinner the next day, considering a number of factors such as weather (so they can serve hot meals on cold days, and cold meals on hot days, for example); surplus foods and garden vegetables on hand, family schedule, including who is home and in charge of cooking; and what kinds of meals have not been prepared for some time.

The Dacyczyns say this type of meal planning, 24 hours in advance, works very well for them. They can thaw frozen foods, soak dried beans, and prepare what's needed for slow cooker meals ahead of time. I think their system has merit, and have often used it myself.

Here are two cautionary points to consider when trying this strategy.

1. Keep your menus varied. One week, while trying a let's-just-use-up-what's-on-hand, last-minute strategy, I ended up preparing the same foods over and over again, to the point where even my children were bored, and that takes some doing. We had three consecutive meals based around some kind of meat and low-fat gravy recipe. I would guess Jim and Amy avoid this scenario, as they consider what they haven't eaten in a while. But I do think it's easy to get lazy with this strategy.

2. Although I don't like rigid meal plans (and neither do the Dacyczyns), there's no reason why you can't draw up some kind of flexible plan. Most people operate better with an outline. Better to be too structured, then relax, than to be too relaxed, then try to structure. In other words, I'd rather have the makings of some great meals on hand and not use them, than have most of what I need and try to make the best of it.

Do 15-Minute Cooking

A friend of mine once said to me, "I can't spend as little on groceries as your family does because I just don't have as much time to cook as you do." Her remark was such a surprise to me that, for a moment, I'm afraid I just stared at her stupidly. As you've read earlier, I spend very little time in the kitchen each day.

Instead, I've developed a system I call "15-minute cooking," one that started years ago when I had a house full of active little ones and no time for much of anything besides the children. Eric was born the day before my thirty-third birthday, and overnight my life changed from one of almost total freedom to being on call 24 hours a day, trying to pacify a very demanding infant. Then came Christian, nineteen months later. By the time Eric turned four, Christian was a wild-man toddler and I also had a baby, Lisa. (That was a circus, I can tell you, and many of you know what I mean.) Michael was working most evenings, so in order to get any kind of a dinner on the table, I found I had to prepare food in very short segments. There was never an extra hour or two available for uninterrupted cooking.

Now, out of years of habit, I still plan most of my recipes and menus so that food can be prepared in two 15-minute sessions a day, one session sometime in the morning and another right before dinner. Obviously, there are many foods you can't cook using this system. You can't make a yeast bread that has to be kneaded and left to rise several times during the day. You can't make complicated entrees or really fancy desserts. Baking time is not included in this system; what we're talking about here is hands-on preparation only. But it's surprising what you *can* prepare in just two 15-minute sessions: home-cooked entrees, side dishes, hot breads, and desserts. With such short time periods required, I've found it much more manageable to assemble a first-rate meal.

Almost every food in this book's recipes section, with the exception of the yeast breads, can be adapted to 15-minute cooking. You might start the vegetable beef soup in the Crock-Pot slow cooker first thing in the morning, for example, and right before dinner make popovers, dice carrot coins, steam broccoli, and prepare a quick fruit dessert for tomorrow night. Next morning, start preparing salmon croquettes and mix up corn bread. Store these in your refrigerator until evening, when you can oven-bake both the salmon and the corn bread, and also slice fresh pineapple and carrot sticks.

The system takes practice, until you get used to overlapping easier-to-prepare dishes with harder ones. You also have to have quick recipes on hand. But as you can imagine, 15-minute cooking is not only healthy, with an emphasis on fresh, nutritious foods, but also a real time-saver. I think we're all more enthusiastic about cooking—especially on the really hectic days—when we know it's going to be fast. That knowledge helps to motivate us to stay home rather than eat out, saving money, too. The 15-minute cooking system works very well for our family. Perhaps it would work well for yours, too.

In summary, organization in meal planning can really run the gamut: plan six months in advance, plan 24 hours in advance, use up your leftovers creatively as you cook, try 15-minute cooking and/or once-a-month cooking, or wing it completely. What's best? That's up to you to decide.

MAKE OR COOK YOUR OWN

In Chapter 2, I listed several ways to save money when buying specific, healthy foods at the store. Another alternative is to save money when *preparing* these same foods. Then, if you buy an item cheaply and also cut some of the preparation costs, your savings are doubled. (Starred items are featured in Recipes.)

Meats and Other Proteins

Let's say, for example, that you've just bought a whole chicken on sale for 59 cents a pound. To save even more in cooking, you can dish up small helpings, or stretch a few ounces a long way in a casserole, ethnic dish, or hearty soup.

Perhaps you can substitute more vegetarian dishes in your diet and make even better use of your food dollars. A variety of healthy foods (from USDA's food pyramid or the basic four food groups) will add up to plenty of complete proteins in the course of a day, even without meat. Jackie Iglehart, former editor of *The Penny Pincher* newsletter, prepares several dishes from cooked beans; she buys 25-pound bags of dry pintos from a food co-op for 41 cents a pound. By teaming beans, homemade breads, grains like brown rice, several vegetables, and fruits, the Igleharts are able to serve low-cost, protein-rich meals for 25 to 50 cents per person.

Don't purchase boneless, skinless chicken breasts at premium prices when you can buy a couple of whole chickens and "make your own" breast portions. I usually place a whole chicken in my Crock-Pot slow cooker; after six to eight hours on the low setting, most meat falls off the bones but the breast pieces are still intact and very tender.

Either way, you'll have several more pounds of meat left over for the same price you would have paid for two measly breast portions.

Cheaper meat tastes better when prepared carefully. Marinades and tenderizers improve both quality and texture, and they need not be expensive. Jill Bond sometimes uses orange or pineapple juice. Mary Ellen, in *Mary Ellen's Helpful Hints*, suggests rubbing a roast with a marinade of vinegar and oil, then letting it stand in the refrigerator for 2 hours before baking. Or slice meat very thinly with a sharp knife, then marinate.

I often cook with a Crock-Pot slow cooker, as mentioned above, because it produces a very tender meat, even from lower-cost cuts. Pressure cookers are another option; these can often be purchased at yard sales for bargain prices. Some cuts of meat, like beef brisket, can be covered with water in a Dutch oven, simmered for 3 or 4 hours until tender, and sliced thinly across the grain.

Dairy Foods

Before you shop the dairy aisle, be aware that there are a number of substitutions you can make at home to save money. Dry milk is often—not always—less costly than liquid, especially if you follow directions carefully and don't load up your drink or recipe with extra powder. Use dry milk powder to make your own sweetened condensed milk* and diet hot chocolate.* Create homemade, low-fat sour cream* in the blender. Another dairy substitute, one for whipped topping,* can also be created from scratch. Homemade orange sherbet* is incredibly easy, nutritious, and cheap.

If you use margarine, you can save considerably by purchasing stick rather than tub versions. And did you know you can make your own inexpensive soft "diet" margarine, one that is lower in fat than the regular version? Using a beater, thoroughly blend a little skim milk into a pound of margarine. You'll have to experiment to see what works best for you, but I've found that I can add almost a cup of skim milk per four sticks. If you prefer butter, substitute stick butter and add milk to that.

You can also create your own yogurt*, a very easy process. You can either use a commercial yogurt maker or simply place small glass jars of liquid yogurt in an oven, pilot light on, overnight. Homemade yogurt can save you money: if milk costs around $2 a gallon, homemade plain yogurt costs about 13 cents a cup. Yogurt is good not only for snacking, but also as an inexpensive, healthy substitute for sour cream and mayonnaise. It can also be drained through cheesecloth to make yogurt cheese.

Breads, Grains, and Cereals

Save on breads, grains, and cereals by cooking a quick, nutritious breakfast. In her booklet *The $30 a Week Grocery Budget*, Donna McKenna lists the following mainstays for breakfast at her house: hot cereals, oatmeal, Cream of Wheat, French toast,* muffins*, pancakes,* and waffles. Jackie Iglehart, former publisher of *The Penny Pincher* newsletter, makes open-faced sandwiches under the broiler, like her "melt-down," an English muffin topped with a thick tomato slice and a thin piece of cheese. Cook hot breakfast cereals overnight in your Crock-Pot slow cooker. Any of these options is much cheaper than cold cereal with milk, and all can be prepared nutritiously.

Jackie Iglehart also recommends using a breadmaker. She claims that, even with an initial outlay of $234 for a top-of-the-line model, her machine paid for itself in a few months and now saves her $500 a year over store-bought bread prices. A baker sells flour and yeast at cost to Jackie, enabling her to produce a loaf of homemade bread for 15 cents. Amy Dacyczyn, author of *The Tightwad Gazette* books, thinks breadmakers are overrated. Instead, Amy uses a food processor or bread bucket to mix dough, then bakes bread as usual in the oven.

Another option is to keep a big batch of yeast bread dough in your refrigerator. The *More-with-Less Cookbook* says any dough with at least one tablespoon of sugar per cup of flour can be stored chilled for up to three days. Spray the top of the kneaded dough with nonfat cooking spray, cover with plastic (first) and a damp cloth, then refrigerate. Punch down as needed. Bring dough to room temperature two hours before baking, and let it rise until doubled, about one and a half to two hours. Bake as usual.

To cut baking costs and eliminate most or all fat, follow the advice in *Secrets of Fat-Free Baking*, an informative recipe book by Sandra Woodruff. Woodruff says you can replace all the fat in cakes, muffins, quick breads, etc. with fruit purees, applesauce, and fruit juices; nonfat yogurt and buttermilk; honey, molasses, jam, corn syrup, and chocolate syrup; prune butter and prune puree; and mashed pumpkin, squash, and sweet potatoes. I've tried this with several recipes and found the "secrets" really work. You won't believe how many loaves of bread I've made from a recycled Halloween pumpkin, and free pumpkin is more nutritious and cheaper than olive oil. (The only drawback is that, in some recipes, you have a lot of sugar. See Resources.)

Here are more fat-reducing—and sometimes money-saving—baking tips:

- Use two egg whites in place of every whole egg. We've found buying whole eggs, then discarding the yolks, is cheaper than buying the prepackaged, low-fat product.
- Add cocoa to recipes calling for chocolate. Three tablespoons plus a little sugar replaces one square of baking chocolate or ¼ cup chocolate pieces.
- Coat pans with nonstick cooking spray rather than buttering and flouring. (This is actually more expensive, but may be worth it in the long run when it comes to health benefits.) Butter-flavored spray is available at most supermarkets.
- Cater to recipes that feature whole grains, such as oatmeal bread, instead of white bread.
- Grind your own wheat into flour. See Resources under "Miscellaneous Products" for ordering information.
- Leave out nuts if they are prohibitively expensive, or use a cheaper variety like Aldi-brand peanuts.
- Bake several items at once—I like to bake muffins at the same time I'm preparing a casserole—and save on energy costs.

If you purchase day-old breads from a bakery outlet, try to stock up on varieties that can be easily reheated. Slightly tough rolls, for example, taste delicious when oven-browned until crispy. Or try my mother-in-law's trick: she heats water in a large pan on the stove, adds a wire basket filled with day-old bread, and steams the bread briefly until it's hot and tender. (Be careful not to let the bread dip into the water; I've done this before.)

Other Foods

BABY FOOD

Breast-feed if you possibly can, and for as long as you can. You can't beat the cost, convenience, or nutrition. La Leche League

International will be glad to answer any questions you may have on nursing, and there's no obligation or fee. See Resources under "Organizations and More."

When your infant is ready for more solid food, check the local library for books on making your own baby food. To tell you the truth, my children went from nursing full-time to slightly bland, mashed-up table food. I sometimes pureed leftovers and froze them in ice cube trays, then microwaved what I needed at the last minute. Most of the time my babies ate right along with us. Of course, caution must be taken: no honey for children under a year old, for example, and no nuts. Popcorn, hot dogs, and grapes must be cut into minuscule pieces. Ask your pediatrician for guidelines.

ICE POPS*

This is a standard snack for us, especially in the summertime. I picked up two Tupperware mold sets at yard sales, and made my money back in two weeks. I often freeze fruit juice, and Frozen Fruit Delight* makes tasty "pops." You can also pour gelatin, pudding, yogurt, Kool-Aid, and just about anything else that's liquid into ice pop molds.

SALAD DRESSINGS

I've found lettuce, homemade salad dressings,* and croutons* team up to make a delicious, inexpensive salad.

SAUCES AND SOUPS

Again, make your own. A basic white sauce*, found in nearly every standard recipe book (including this one), takes about 5 minutes. From the parent recipe you can create cheese sauce, gravy*, cream of mushroom soup, and a number of variations, none of them high in fat or calories.

Broth is another commodity that's cheap and simple: add a little extra water to the roast or chicken you're baking, collect the liquid when you're finished, and skim off the extra fat. (If you refrigerate the broth, fat solidifies at the top and is easily removed.) I freeze excess defatted broth and always have a supply on hand. Use it in homemade gravies, or start a soup pot in the freezer; when there's enough liquid, vegetables, and meat, you're ready to simmer up a stew.

SEASONINGS

You may want to purchase spices at discount stores or drugstores, or in bulk from a co-op, warehouse, or health food store, where they are almost always cheaper than the supermarket. But do try the recipe for taco seasoning* in Recipes!

SYRUP

Make your own low-fat maple-flavored pancake syrup* and save at least 75% over store cost. Or try my delicious pancakes,* so moist they taste scrumptious with a simple dusting of powdered sugar.

Drinks

If my children have reached their daily quota of milk products, I serve them orange juice for dinner. (It beats soda and Kool-Aid, which we used to have more often.) We make orange juice from frozen concentrate as Aldi's brand is much cheaper than ready-made; compare prices in your area for the best buy.

We also drink ice water between meals, as "seconds" at meals, and in the car when we're out and about. Sometimes on hot summer days, we fill a clean recycled milk jug two-thirds full of water, freeze it, and take it along on a trip. The melting water stays icy cold for a few hours.

We recently bought a water filter, one that fastens over the faucet and blocks a number of harmful ingredients from coming through, at Wal-Mart. (This is especially helpful for me, as I am highly allergic to chlorine.) Though replacement filters are expensive, we ration our drinking water carefully and think we have been a little healthier since changing to filtered water.

Here's an idea for stretching coffee from Larry Roth, the author of several books on saving money. He takes the used grinds from a Mr. Coffee–type coffeemaker, lets them cool, refrigerates, then adds new coffee to the existing grounds. Larry uses three and a half spoons for the first pot, and, for each subsequent pot, adds two and a half spoons until the filter is full. After that, he throws it all out and starts over. Larry says he can't tell any difference in the taste. For a gourmet flavored coffee, try adding a pinch of salt, a little vanilla, or some cinnamon.

Also see the Recipe Index under "Drinks" for more ideas.

In summary, as you trim your family's grocery bill, be on the lookout for ways to cut costs through preparing food and drinks yourself. It's an easy way to compound your savings.

GARDEN

We planted our first real garden a few years ago, and the whole experience was a dismal one. While the neighbors' tomato plants yielded dozens of firm, delicious fruit, our scraggly vines produced about ten. And a woodchuck from the nearby woods ate half of them. Our beans were so badly chewed we didn't get a single pod. Obviously we have much to learn about gardening.

Cooperative Extension Services

Thankfully, there is help. I called our land grant university's extension service (Cooperative Extension Service). Off-campus faculty, so I'm told, translate the teaching and research of the university into workable knowledge for people of the state. When I spoke with the horticulture specialist at the University of Missouri, I was impressed with the scope of the program.

He sent me a listing of sample publications—most of them free or costing 25 to 50 cents each—on topics as varied as a vegetable planting calendar, mulching, soil preparation, how to grow specific fruits and vegetables, making your own compost bins, and dozens more. Some of the pamphlets are very specific, such as "Home Production of Black Walnuts and Nut Meats." In short, your nearby Cooperative Extension Service (CES) should have just about everything you need to know regarding gardening and related topics. If you are unsure how to find such a program, refer to Resources under "Organizations and More."

Gardening Books and Publications

A trip to the library or an online search can supply you with plenty of reading material: gardening magazines, or classics like *Crockett's Victory Gardens* (Little, Brown & Co.), *Square Foot Gardening* (Rodale Press) tell you how to make the most of your garden space and conserve water and labor at the same time. *Gardening by Mail* (Houghton Mifflin Co.) is a sourcebook that lists what's available to you through mail order.

Gardening centers and nurseries may also feature a rack of good books. *All About Vegetables*, an Ortho publication, was recommended to me by horticulturists at the Missouri Botanical Gardens. Very specific sources like this one, as well as organic gardening magazines, are likely to be found at home and garden centers. Salespeople are usually knowledgeable and truly willing to help, and you can take advantage of their expertise.

And while you're at such a store, peek into the encyclopedic *Ortho Problem Solver*, with answers to—and illustrations of—2,000 garden problems; many home and garden centers share their copy as a service to customers.

If you're often on the move, consider container gardening. Jackie Iglehart, former publisher of *The Penny Pincher* newsletter, has grown not only basic crops like tomatoes, but even fruit trees, in portable containers. This has given her family the advantage of home-grown produce even in the midst of several moves all over the country.

Finally, you might check out the possibility of sharing garden space with a neighbor. Our neighbor Diana planted a large garden last year in her backyard, and our children helped her seed and weed. In return, we shared the harvest.

Garden Clubs

Perhaps you would enjoy a more cooperative effort in your gardening. If so, local garden clubs may be the answer. The national headquarters of the National Council of State Garden Clubs has chapters in all fifty states and another in the District of Columbia, and its 264,000+ members work together on a number of different projects, vegetable gardening included. Study courses are offered to members. *The National Gardener* magazine, leadership training, flower shows, a scholarship fund, and environmental activism are only a few of the many benefits available. To locate a chapter near you, see Resources, "Organizations and More."

You can organize your own informal "club" to share garden produce. I once spoke at a church where members with gardens brought their surplus fruits and vegetables and left them, each week, on a designated table. Anyone was free to both bring and take away this produce.

Our family continues to try gardening. This past year, our youngest daughter, Mary, was given a number of wilted vegetable seedlings and planted them in our neighbor Diana's now-vacant garden space. We had a nice yield of a few tomatoes in late summer, and more veggies later in the fall. We're still learning.

PRESERVE YOUR FOOD

Let's assume that you've had a great yield on your garden (better than mine, anyway), and you have bushels of food to process. Or you've been to the farmers' market and returned home with a couple of crates of bargain tomatoes and apples. What's next?

There's no point in my lecturing at length on the fine points of canning, freezing, and otherwise preserving foods, since I have little firsthand experience. So let me put you in touch with advice from some real experts.

First, at the risk of being repetitive, contact your local Cooperative Extension Service when you're ready to put away food. The University of Illinois Cooperative Extension Service sent me an inch-thick packet of canning and freezing fact sheets covering every topic imaginable: "Freezer Storage Chart," "Reduced and Sugar-Free Jams, Jellies, and Preserves," and "Using Home-Preserved Foods Safely" are just a few of the varied titles. You can also find very specific information on processing particular foods, from tomatillos to pawpaws to beef jerky—and more common foods, too, of course. Again, most of this information is free or near-free, and very much up-to-date. Guidelines for canning tomatoes, for example, have changed in the last few years, and a CES in your area can tell you exactly how and why.

Freezing

Nearly every standard cookbook explains the basics of freezing foods. If you pre-prepare meals through once-a-month or Mega-cooking (and already have one of the handbooks on hand), consult *Once-a-Month Cooking* and/or *Mega-Cooking* for ideas on safely freezing foods. Jill Bond, in *Mega-Cooking*, devotes an entire chapter to "Storing It All Away." Here are some of her suggestions.

1. Freeze carefully. Jill uses zippered, heavy-duty freezer bags and plastic containers with tight seals. She also recommends foil, clear plastic wrap, and freezer wrap applied generously and overlapped. (Or, as was mentioned earlier, use the liners from boxed cereal.)
2. Label your food, including date and contents.
3. Keep an inventory of foods in your freezer. Jill prefers a write-and-wipe board, where items are erased as they're taken out of the freezer and added as they're put in.

4. Freeze most of your foods in meal-size portions. An exception to this is an item like blueberries, which can be frozen in a single layer on a cookie sheet, bagged later, and then retrieved in the quantity needed.

Canning

Several years ago, under a friend's watchful eye, I canned a big batch of pears and homemade applesauce from fruit I'd gleaned. This was my first experience with canning, and I really enjoyed it. In spite of the hard work, sweat, and sore fingers from all that peeling, there was something very satisfying about the end product, dozens of jars of food on the shelf in my cupboards.

Canning really isn't difficult or expensive, say Pat Edwards of *Cheap Eating* and Amy Dacyczyn of *The Tightwad Gazette* books. It does require caution, good equipment, and a willingness to look for the best buys. You'll need canning jars (often available at yard or estate sales) in perfect condition, and basics like a colander, ladle, and funnel. For safety's sake, buy new lids; purchase them at salvage stores, or watch for sales. Many people prefer a pressure canner instead of a regular canner, as it makes the process much quicker and more enjoyable. It's very possible that you can buy quality used or discounted equipment, as well as share with friends, and considerably cut your investment costs.[3]

Why can when you have freezer space available? You and your family may prefer the taste. Amy Dacyczyn likes the immediacy of canned foods—as opposed to searching in the bottom of the freezer—and having canning as an option if extra food is available and the freezer's full. She also points out that canned goods make nice gifts; freezer foods don't fare too well under the Christmas tree.

Since this topic has to be either brief or incredibly detailed (and I don't think I'll get into pickling, drying, smoking, or salting foods at all), I'll close with recommendations from my two experts for more advice in the form of two books: *Ball Blue Book Guide to Home Canning, Freezing, and Dehydration* and *Putting Food By*. See Resources.

GLEAN

There is much free and low-cost food available, and often it's only a matter of finding and gleaning it.

For example, my sister-in-law Joan once worked out a deal with a local supermarket. The produce department boxed up damaged produce and called Joan, who picked it up for free. A few years ago, when Joan came for a visit, she brought along three crates of cucumbers and a huge box of all sorts of fruits, including strawberries, as a gift. And she still had plenty left over for her own family.

A major vegetable company owns fields near my hometown and, after harvest, allows anyone interested to glean leftover potatoes or green beans. A family friend, Eunice, used to pick a year's worth of free beans and can 100 quarts or more each summer. Eunice says she has salvaged vegetables from other fields as well, even when on vacation. She checks at local grain elevators to learn harvest days, or simply stops to ask a farmer's permission to glean.

Pass the word around your neighborhood that you'd be glad to take—and give—surplus food. One friend and I occasionally trade leftovers: her family tires of the big roast they cooked on Sunday, and we trade some of their meat for a loaf of my homemade bread. When a neighbor moved out of state and had to leave behind the contents of her well-stocked refrigerator and freezer, she asked another friend and me to gather up the goods and divide them between us. Last summer we shared extra vegetables from my sister-in-law with our neighbors.

Keep your eyes open for salvageable food that's going to waste. I've always loved to run and walk, and used to make it a point to try different routes. One autumn day several years ago, I noticed an apple tree laden with fruit; soon much of it lay on the lawn. Several more pass-bys confirmed that no one was picking the apples. Later that week, I stopped and asked the owner if he would mind if I cleaned up his yard in exchange for apples. He was delighted.

My two little boys and I made numerous trips to that man's backyard. We collected so many apples that I canned several batches of applesauce and gave some away as Christmas presents. I sold dozens of bags of fruit to fellow workers. And we had enough apples, stored in a cool closet and eating at least four a day, to last us into January.

Another autumn, I was able to locate a pear tree and glean pears from a busy owner (the one who supplied pears for canning). I have also harvested several pounds of free hickory nuts.

It has been satisfying to me, through the years, to have gleaned a great deal of no-cost fruits, vegetables, and nuts to help feed my family, and also to have kept the food from going to waste.

BENEFIT FROM GOVERNMENT PROGRAMS

Your taxes help support a number of different food programs, and you may need to take advantage of some of them when times are exceptionally hard.

As of this writing, USDA's Food and Consumer Service (FCS) provides these services: Food Stamp Program; Special Supplemental Nutrition Program for Women, Infants, and Children (WIC); National School Lunch Program; School Breakfast Program; Summer Food Service Program; The Emergency Food Assistance Program (TEFAP); Child and Adult Care Food Program; The WIC Farmers Market Nutrition Program; Commodity Supplemental Food Program; Special Milk Program; Food Distribution Program on Indian Reservations and the Trust Territories; Nutrition Program for the Elderly; and Commodity Distribution to Charitable Institutions and to Soup Kitchens and Food Banks.

Your first step should be a call to the U.S. Department of Agriculture's Food and Consumer Service to learn about what's currently available, as programs may have changed considerably since this writing. You can find the local number in the blue pages of your phone book.

EAT SENSIBLY

As we discussed in the introduction, there is a difference of opinion as to what it means to eat sensibly. My family and I are trying to take a healthy middle ground, one of cutting back on fat, sugar, and fatty meats, yet increasing our intake of fruits and vegetables, fiber, and whole foods.

We've found that, over time, our food bills have gone down in some areas, as we buy much less meat, especially more expensive beef cuts, and fewer convenience foods. On the other hand, our produce bill alone averages between $15 and $20 a week. It takes a lot of fruits and vegetables to feed six of us "five a day," as the American Cancer Society recommends. Still, all of this is an investment in good health. I have seen a reduction in the number of colds and sick days we've all experienced, and I believe this is directly related to our new and improved way of eating. Also, as some wise person put it, spending a few extra dollars a week on healthy food is a lot cheaper than bypass surgery.

Michael and I think of our new shopping and cooking strategies as a lifestyle change rather than a diet. But for those of you who are officially dieting, here's some advice.

- Eat plenty of fresh, seasonal fruit and vegetables.
- Exercise to cut your appetite.
- Make your own diet meals by saving a variety of healthy leftovers in containers in the freezer, then reheating.
- Cook extra meat and slice thinly for a delicious diet lunch. Not only is the flavor much better, but you will also avoid the high-fat content of most packaged lunch meats.
- Take low-calorie snacks to work with you rather than facing the temptation of the vending machine.
- If you're craving sweets, have a small portion of a homemade treat instead of buying expensive "diet" desserts.
- Drink lots of water or iced tea. For those who crave diet sodas, buy cans by the case.
- Consider forming or joining a support group rather than going to a costly weight loss clinic.
- Think of your dieting as a long-term health benefit rather than a short-term deprivation.

Are you amazed, as I was, to learn of so many ways to save money on groceries? Use some or all of these strategies—wherever you live, whatever your circumstances—and you really can feed your family for $12 a day.

Just how does a family go about implementing these positive changes? The next chapter explains.

NOTES

1. and 2. From "Once-A-Month Cooking," an article by Mimi Wilson and Mary Beth Lagerborg in *Focus on the Family Magazine*, April 1992, P.O. Box 35500, Colorado Springs, Colorado 80935-3550. See Resources for information about the *Once-A-Month Cooking* book.

3. To learn more about canning, refer to *The Tightwad Gazette* books by Amy Dacyczyn, and Pat Edwards's book, *Cheap Eating*. See Resources.

CHAPTER 4

How Do I Ever Manage to Do All This?

Now that you've read several chapters, are you inspired enough to begin cutting back on your grocery bills? Or are you discouraged? Does it all seem too complicated and time-consuming?

Not long ago I attended a meeting where the speaker was supposed to motivate the rest of us to get organized. Unfortunately, just the opposite resulted. We all looked around rather hopelessly at each other, wondering how in the world we could ever accomplish what this woman did in a single day.

I hope you don't feel the same way about saving money on food. It does take time and organization, especially at first. But I guarantee that you can do it, once you find your own system, and save substantially in a relatively painless way.

In order to demonstrate this a little more clearly, let me paint a hypothetical picture for you. Penny Price will be my make-believe person, the main shopper and meal planner for the Price family. Her husband, John, and three school-age children—Susan, Steve, and Danny—are also involved. Let's say that Penny has read this book and decided it's time to take action. We'll follow her and her family through a year and observe the changes they make in their lifestyle.

January 2
Penny shops as usual at her favorite store. She carries along a small notebook and jots down prices on stock-up items like eggs, skim milk, and whole-grain bread. Penny takes a little longer than usual to

check out store and generic brands and also writes down their cost in her notebook.

January 9

This week, Penny stops by a nearby grocery store, one she seldom frequents simply out of habit. As she records prices in her notebook, she's surprised to find some items significantly cheaper than those at her usual store. She also discovers an out-of-the-way bin where marked-down meat is stored. Penny learns from the meat manager that surplus cuts are placed in the bin each morning, often at a 50% savings. While there, she stocks up on ketchup and oats, on sale at an exceptionally good price.

January 16

Penny visits a membership warehouse club with her price book. Cost-per-ounce signs help her decide whether buying in bulk would really save money. She concludes that some purchases, like dry cereal, cheese, and orange juice, are definitely cheaper at the warehouse, and she resolves to shop there once a month.

January 23

At the breakfast table the morning before shopping, Penny compares two grocery store flyers and notes several items she needs on sale at National. She checks her price book and sees that the "loss leader" foods are a good buy, cheaper than any other prices in the area. She does all her shopping at National this week.

January 30

Penny checks out a meat market just across from the mall, right on her way home from other errands. She speaks with the butcher and gets some good advice on bargain cuts of meat and how to cook them. Penny buys chicken leg quarters on sale, several pounds at a considerable savings. She asks the butcher to wrap the poultry in two-pound packages and freezes all but one package for future use.

February 6

Susan has taken an interest in couponing and now clips several coupons from the Sunday paper, arranging them in an envelope. As Penny goes through supermarket flyers this week, she matches several sale items with Susan's coupons for even greater savings. She plans to shop at A&P, as it offers the best buys on what she needs, as well as double coupons.

February 13

Penny takes a critical look at the kinds of goods she's been buying and decides to eliminate several convenience foods. This week, she purchases store brand tea bags rather than a six-pack of soda, bulk buy raisins instead of lunch-size packages, and generic toasted oats in place of name brand cereal.

February 20

John and the children sit down together and read through the book *Square Foot Gardening.* Some online research and a visit to the library provide even more valuable information, including some gardening magazines and *Gardening by Mail*, a sourcebook on where to order supplies. Once they decide on the garden's layout, Danny and John plan to start seedlings in a warm, sunny corner of their walkout basement.

February 27

The Prices have invited the Aldens for Saturday brunch and plan a special "theme meal" with pancakes as the main dish. John prepares a huge batch of oatmeal pancakes the night before, first adding bananas, nuts, chocolate chips, and bits of low-fat cheese to four separate bowls of batter. When the Aldens arrive, a buffet is ready with syrup, honey, fruit sauce, yogurt, and ice milk as complements. The two families can't remember ever having so much fun at a company meal.

March 5

Penny finds some intriguing low-fat recipes and decides to give them a try. First she whips up an easy nonfat French salad dressing. She makes her own croutons and bread pudding, using leftover whole-wheat bread ends. She tries a basic white sauce recipe, adding mushrooms, to substitute for canned soup in the chicken casserole she's serving tonight. And she bakes a triple batch of applesauce gingerbread cake from scratch in less time than it takes to put together a single cake mix. Penny's hour in the kitchen saves the Price family about $15 *and* several grams of fat per person.

March 12

John decides to "brown bag" three times a week instead of eating lunch out. Susan, Steve, and Danny begin packing their own lunchboxes on the same days. John assembles barbecued chicken sandwiches, low-fat cheese slices, air-popped popcorn, carrot sticks with nonfat dip, raisins, pretzels, crackers, leftovers of all kinds, and homemade raspberry yogurt. The Prices estimate they can bank at least $24 weekly by bringing their own healthy food from home instead of purchasing noontime meals.

March 19

John starts a new system for making coffee, a necessary expense in the Price household. He mixes grounds from the day before with fresh ones for a 50% savings. Penny cuts back to two cups of coffee a day and plans to drink more water instead.

March 26

One brisk weekend day, Penny is in the mood for homemade bread. She tries a 90-minute recipe (see Cinnamon Yeast Bread, in Recipes) and bakes four loaves. The children help, forming their own smaller dough balls, rolling them out, and sprinkling on cinnamon and sugar. Danny loves the taste of hot-out-of-the-oven bread so much that he asks to make it again soon. In a few weeks he is able to turn out loaves from start to finish all by himself.

April 2

Penny visits the membership warehouse club again after an absence of several weeks. She is a smarter buyer this time around, and doesn't succumb, as she did during her first visit, to the temptations of boxed doughnuts and ready-made cheesecake. For breakfast the next morning Penny whips up a batch of healthy bran muffins and a big batch of low-fat orange sherbet for dinner dessert. By not buying doughnuts and cheesecake and substituting healthier, homemade sweets, Penny saves more than $8 on two items alone.

April 9

Penny and John have made it a point to talk more frequently with Susan, Steve, and Danny about nutrition, and have also been buying and eating healthier foods. When the children arrive home from school now, they often fill up on celery with low-fat cream cheese, orange juice ice pops, or dry toasted oat cereal mixed with raisins. Fresh fruit has also become a favorite snack.

April 16

By now Penny is quite a pro at using up leftovers, and the Prices waste very little food. Their freezer holds a large plastic container where leftover bits of meat, vegetables, and broth accumulate until there is enough for a kettle of soup or stew. Penny checks the refrigerator and cupboard shelves at least twice a week for odds and ends. Those foods that can't be made into soup are served at Thursday night dinner, buffet-style.

April 23

John goes shopping this week, checking out a new produce stand on his way home from work. The manager is eager for business and talks with John for a few minutes about seasonal fruit and other bargains. Bananas are on special, six pounds for $1. John buys $10 worth of fruit, including several bunches of bananas.

April 30

After a week of eating bananas twice a day, the Prices decide to freeze the excess. Some bananas are skewered on wood sticks and dipped in chocolate syrup, then wrapped in wax paper. The rest are pureed with a little lemon juice in a blender and frozen in 2-cup containers, to be used later in banana bread.

May 7

Penny and John sit down together and do some serious meal planning. They make a simple list of thirty meals that nearly everyone in the family enjoys. Steve constructs a chart and helps arrange meals for the next month, projecting ahead for days when the family will eat out and planning to be flexible as needed. In the meantime, Penny tries the 24-hour-in-advance plan, deciding on dinner meals the night before she prepares them.

May 14

The neighbors down the street have joined a commercial exchange organization and tell the Prices about bartering. After careful consideration, John and Penny decide against joining. Instead, they contact several close friends and propose an informal kind of arrangement: any family who has a surplus will try to swap with another family who has a need. Penny agrees in advance to barter garden vegetables for the use of another family's pressure canner.

May 21

The Prices make a joint decision to budget the amount of money spent for eating out together. After a couple of weeks of casually checking out restaurant coupons, they have decided that takeout pizza is their best bet. It's about half the cost of dining at their favorite steakhouse. They'll still splurge occasionally, of course. But by saving their restaurant money in a piggy bank, they'll soon have the extra cash they need to buy a family membership at the local pool this summer.

May 28

Penny and John have gradually made some major changes in their diet, and are thinner and more fit than they were six months ago. Everyone now eats less red meat and more beans, brown rice, and whole-wheat pasta; less sugary desserts and more nutritious alternatives. As they've cut their food bill, Penny and John have also cut their cholesterol levels and their weight.

June 4

It's vegetable-planting time. One warm Saturday the Prices bring seedlings up from the basement and ready the soil in their garden plot. They barter the use of a neighbor's tiller; in exchange, John and Steve will restack the man's disorganized firewood. The Prices are also able to locate fertilizer and some needed tools on sale at a nearby nursery. The garden is planted by dinnertime.

June 11

John, head gardener of the family, visits the University of Missouri's Cooperative Extension Service. He wants to get the latest information on "integrated pest management" so the Prices won't have to spend money on—and face health risks from—pesticides. John speaks in person with an expert adviser. He also takes home some free brochures on ways to maximize vegetable growth, build his own compost pile, and have the garden soil tested.

June 18

John, Penny, and the children spend a Saturday morning at a pick-your-own strawberry patch. They've come at the end of the season and are able to glean berries at half the usual cost. The family picks enough to have plenty of homemade jam, strawberry desserts, and plain, delicious snacks.

June 25

Sunday is a perfect summer day, and the Price family decide to spend the afternoon at the zoo. Their usual custom is to eat the food stand's overpriced hot dogs, popcorn, and soda. Today they pack a picnic instead. The $35 designated for lunch is used to purchase books at the zoo's gift shop.

July 2

Three of the Prices have birthdays this month, and Penny decides to bake the cakes herself. She makes a triple batch of Fudge Brownies (see Recipes) and freezes three finished sheet cakes. Next comes a triple batch of frosting—and again, two containers are frozen. Thanks to advance preparation, each cake will require less than 20 minutes for final assembly.

July 9

The garden is growing nicely and the first crop of string beans comes in. The Prices cook a big batch for supper, using defatted ham broth for flavoring. As other produce ripens over the course of the summer, Penny contacts her friend about the swap they had agreed to earlier: use of a pressure canner in exchange for some vegetables. Now the family will be able to put up several quarts each of beans, peas, and tomatoes themselves.

July 16

Penny learns that several church friends are organizing a co-op buying club. She attends an organizational meeting and carefully examines the supplier's catalog. For about an hour's worth of work each month, Penny can purchase some products at a real savings, including bulk yeast, spices, low-fat cheese, and whole-wheat flour. She joins the co-op.

July 23

John, hungry for something home-baked, rescues pureed bananas and frozen strawberries from the freezer. A couple of hours later he's taking three large, steaming loaves of banana-berry bread from the oven. The Prices enjoy one loaf that night and generous slices for lunch the next two days.

July 30

Penny's brother and his family are spending the weekend and the Prices intend to entertain them in style. Penny brings out lasagna and homemade French bread from the freezer, and makes a quick Five-Minute Chocolate Custard Pie (see Recipes) for Friday night's meal. Saturday features a barbecue with grilled marinated chicken, corn on the cob, and fresh garden vegetables. Sunday dinner is turkey with all the trimmings. Penny's brother and sister-in-law enjoy the home-cooked meals and are convinced their relatives have spent a fortune to feed them. (The Prices don't tell them otherwise.)

August 6

Susan has become so skilled at using coupons that, shopping with her mother, she's able to save more than $7 at the store this week. Penny has promised that her daughter can bank any money saved on coupons, so Susan is especially attentive to good deals. She has even set up a coupon exchange box at the library and checks it regularly.

August 13

John has just learned about a new farmers' market in the city, a 30-minute drive from home. Word has it that farmers there sell their goods at tremendous savings toward the end of the day. The Price family makes a trip downtown to the zoo, then later stop by the market. They arrive late afternoon Saturday and, sure enough, come away with two large crates of fresh produce for a fraction of normal supermarket prices.

August 20

Using some of the money they've saved on groceries, the Prices have purchased a used chest-type freezer. Penny has collected garage sale containers all summer and has quite a stockpile. Vegetables and fruits from the farmers' market on Saturday are carefully sorted, processed, and frozen. Between the market's produce and their own garden's yield, the Price freezer is nearly full.

August 27

A librarian approaches Susan as she checks her coupon trading box: has she heard about refunding? The librarian locates the name and address of *Refund Express*. Susan sends for a sample copy. She is amazed to receive a thick newsprint magazine filled with inspiring stories, numbers to call for free products, and hundreds of ads where swaps can be made for coupons and refund offers. Susan signs up as a subscriber.

September 3

It's taken the Prices eight months, but their weekly grocery bill is now down to about $85, around $12 a day. John and Penny's usual routine involves a trip to the membership warehouse club the first week of each month, where they stock up on lower-cost bulk items. The next three weeks Penny shops at one of two grocery stores, depending on which has the best specials and the best match-up with Susan's coupons. Penny also stops by the meat market occasionally. The produce stand, right on her way to one of the supermarkets, is usually so much cheaper that she often makes a quick run in for fresh fruits and vegetables.

September 10

Steve, riding his bike around the block, has noticed a neighbor's pear tree. Several trips by confirm that no one is picking the fruit. With Penny's approval, Steve leaves a note on the neighbor's door politely requesting that he be allowed to pick the pears. He gets a call the next day from an elderly man who's happy to have his fruit gleaned. Steve stops by one day after school and cleans the man's yard, carefully picking up the grounded pears that are salvageable. The rotted ones are hauled home to the family compost pile. Dozens are eaten for snacks. And the rest Steve sells door to door, collecting quite a sum for his "new bike" fund.

September 17

While out looking for garage sales, Penny notices a day-old-bread store and stops to investigate. The prices are excellent. She stocks up on whole-grain bagels, dinner rolls, hamburger buns, and several loaves of oat bread. Penny freezes some breads and oven-toasts bagels. The rest are steamed over a kettle of hot water to almost-fresh quality.

September 24

The Prices have "put out the word" throughout their neighborhood that they will gladly accept any free food or goods, especially those that might otherwise go to waste. Soon friends are calling them: a hunter who has extra venison to share, a gardener who doesn't want to process all of her bumper tomato crop. The Prices graciously follow up with homemade bread loaves as thank-yous.

October 1

Autumn weather has everyone in the mood to pick apples. John, Penny, Susan, Steve, and Danny make a day of it at a nearby orchard, gathering over 50 pounds of fruit. They save about 70% compared to normal supermarket prices and have a wonderful time as well. The orchard owner supplies all three children with free small pumpkins as a bonus. Best of all, the whole family enjoys a wagon ride behind the farmer's tractor.

October 8

Penny has just read *Once-a-Month Cooking* and decides to try two weeks' worth of shopping plans and menus. She sets aside a Saturday morning for shopping and a Sunday afternoon and evening for cooking. The system works very well. Penny is surprised at how much is accomplished in a short time, and soon she has fourteen entrees ready in the freezer. In a few months, she'll try Mega-cooking, then decide which system works best for the Price family.

October 15

Penny and the children prepare for Halloween a little early this year. Together, they create an enormous batch of cookie dough and a triple recipe of caramel corn. Steve bags the caramel corn for his school party, and also helps Penny roll out dough and cut cookies. Susan and Danny frost and decorate little pumpkin-shaped sugar cookies. The children don't mind their chores since the rewards— bites of treats—are definitely worth the work.

October 22

Susan wants to have a few friends over for dinner and a sleepover. The Prices agree, and set a $15 spending limit. No problem, Susan says. She scans her bulging coupon collection and pulls out several to use at a store offering double savings. She buys bread, deli meat packages, cheese, and soda on sale. With her coupons, they're less than half the original cost. Susan also buys plain white napkins and plates, and glues on handmade autumn motifs. The menu for the eight friends includes turkey-and-cheese sandwiches on buns, corn chips with homemade dip, carrot sticks, pretzels, caramel corn, cookies, and soda, all at a total cost of $15.68. (Hey, we can't eat perfectly healthy foods all the time!)

October 29

John and the boys buy a large pumpkin from the produce stand and carve it for Halloween. The seeds are washed, dried, and oven-roasted. In a day or two the pumpkin itself will be cut into pieces, slow-cooked, and pureed in the food processor. Penny will make a few pies and have plenty left over to pop in the freezer.

November 5

Halloween candy is on sale, so Penny purchases several large bags. She knows from experience that discounted candy bars and M&Ms are often cheaper than baking chips. Penny freezes all the goodies in hidden reaches so no one will be overly tempted. Over the next few months she will have a large cache of both treats and baking chocolate—for the children, of course.

November 12

Thanksgiving is two weeks away and turkeys are on sale at the supermarket. Penny relies on her stockpile of other foods and spends most of the grocery budget on meat. She buys a whole turkey at 39 cents a pound and freezes it. She also invests in extra cranberries, reduced-fat margarine, whipped topping, and other sale items.

November 19

Steve, the entrepreneur of the family, has found another source of income: nuts. While exploring a family friend's "back 40," he's located an out-of-the-way pecan tree. Steve gets permission to gather over a bushel and spends a few hours shelling pecans. Penny and several neighbors buy large containers full of nuts for $5 each, still a good savings over store prices. Steve soon has another $35 to put in the bank. At this rate he'll have enough money for his new bike by spring.

November 26

As the Prices celebrate Thanksgiving, they are truly thankful to God for their bountiful harvest of food. Penny has bought a second, fresh turkey and made her own low-fat stuffing and gravy. The menu also includes peas and potatoes from the garden. Using some of

Steve's pecans, Susan and Danny have baked a banana-nut loaf. John's special offering is his own cranberry relish; Penny's, a homemade pumpkin pie. The meal has been a real cooperative effort. But the results are outstanding in both savings and taste.

December 3
Penny and a group of friends meet for an informal potluck at the Prices' house. The discussion turns to the astronomical cost of feeding a family, and Penny shares some of the strategies she's learned in the past year. Three women agree to try an informal swap of Christmas cookies next week in an effort to save both time and money. The Prices, the Aldens, and the Fergusons will each bake triple batches of three different recipes, delivering one batch of each to the others' homes.

December 10
John is in the mood for Christmas shopping. Instead of heading for the mall, the family brainstorms some ideas for homemade presents. Danny wants to give his own special cinnamon yeast bread. Susan decides to make coupon holders, each with 100 coupons filed alphabetically inside. Steve plans to share jars of canned pears, the ones he foraged from a neighbor three months earlier. John and Penny will buy some items, of course. But for friends and co-workers, they decide to give assorted homemade muffins. They estimate a savings of at least $300 over the previous year, when most of their gifts averaged $35 per person.

December 17
Penny has budgeted ahead, and plans to take advantage of holiday sales. The meat market has just advertised whole hams at half price, so she buys two. Susan is enthusiastically clipping coupons; many more are available during the holiday season. Between sales and double coupons, the Prices' grocery bill totals less than half of the regular cost of food.

December 24
Penny and John exchange Christmas gifts shortly after the children are in bed for the night. Along with a few romantic offerings, John has also written out a coupon—good for five home-baked loaves of bread each week of the new year—for Penny (and the family). Penny can't

decide which she likes better, her new perfume or that valuable coupon.

December 31

As the new year rolls in, the Prices make a resolution: to save even more this year than last. They have learned much about ways to conserve the food dollar. Now they'll try their hand at other means of cutting back. Their goal is a family vacation to a ski lodge over the holidays next December. With the money they save, they'll be able to do it.

And so Penny, John, Susan, Steve, and Danny live happily ever after. And it is a fairy tale, I admit; real life seldom runs so smoothly. But the Prices cut healthy food costs in a very realistic way, one step at a time, one new strategy each week. That's what Michael and I have done, and it works. We actually practice much of what the Prices supposedly tried, and I know of many others who manage to accomplish this and much more. The composite picture is fictional but certainly possible.

The idea of my make-believe story is to inspire you. Wouldn't it be fun to write your own true story this year?

CHAPTER 5

"I Can't Save Money on Groceries Because . . ."

The story of Penny Price is behind us now, and it's time to face reality. Do you think that, for you and your family, it's impossible to spend as little as $12 a day for healthy foods? Your groceries may cost considerably more than $84 a week, but you have a good excuse, right? Then let's talk about it. Please fill in the blank below:

"I can't save money on groceries because ———."

Now allow me to anticipate some of your answers and offer some suggestions. Remember, these are just *suggestions*. You should decide which, if any, work best as a solution to your particular problem.

"I can't save money on groceries because I'm too tired to cook and rely on convenience foods for most of my meals."

- Do once-a-month or Mega-cooking on a weekend (or some other time when you're more rested) and make your own convenience foods, stockpiled in the freezer.
- Try some of the recipes in the next chapter. Most dishes can be prepared in 15 to 30 minutes or less.
- Rely more heavily on time-saving devices—such as a Crock-Pot slow cooker, breadmaker, pressure cooker, or food processor—to make cooking faster.
- Menu plan carefully to allow for quick, easy homemade meals on nights when you know you'll be most tired.
- Try 15-minute cooking—my own system for cooking 15 minutes

early in the morning (or right after dinner the night before), then 15 minutes just before dinner—for delicious, home-cooked meals. See Resources.

"I can't save money on groceries because I'm on a restricted diet and have to pay more for special foods."

For a low-fat and low-cholesterol diet:
- Calculate the number of grams of fat in the foods you eat, then devise an inexpensive diet with no more than 30% of total calories from fat. If, for example, you need 2,000 calories a day to maintain your weight, take 30% x 2,000 = 600 calories; 9 calories per gram of fat = 67 grams of total fat per day. Make healthy, cheap menu choices that keep your fat intake under 30% of your total daily calories (in this case, 67 grams).
- Combine double coupons with supermarket sales, and stock up on low-fat versions of margarine, sour cream, cheese, and other staples when they're cheapest.
- Serve just a little of the "real stuff." It's worth it to me to have a teaspoon of real sour cream rather than a tablespoon of the low-fat version, and the fat content is about the same. Nonfat and low-fat products usually cost much more than their "regular" counterparts.
- Do your own baking, but apply these fat- and cholesterol-cutting rules: For cakes and soft-drop cookies, use no more than 2 tablespoons of fat per cup of flour. For muffins, quick breads, and biscuits, use no more than 1 to 2 tablespoons of fat per cup of flour. See other baking suggestions in Chapter 3 under "Make and Cook Your Own: Breads, Grains, and Cereals."

For a diabetic diet:
- See the next chapter for recipes reprinted from *Healthy Exchanges* newsletters. If you like what you try, I highly recommend buying the *Healthy Exchanges* cookbooks. See Resources.
- Also check out the library for a selection of cookbooks for people with diabetes.

For healthier eating in general:
- Eat smaller quantities of healthy foods. As silly as that sounds, it is perhaps the most surefire way to lose weight.

- Bulk buy olive oil, brown rice, dry beans, and other healthy foods from a membership warehouse club or a co-op.
- Think of meat as a side dish, and serve only small portions. Cook more chicken and turkey. Fortunately, both are usually cheaper than beef or pork.
- Learn to eat fish. Buy seafood that is currently in season. Better yet, take up fishing.
- Fill up on fresh fruits and vegetables, purchased in season from supermarket sales, produce stands, or farmers' markets.
- Serve beans. The *More-with-Less Cookbook* features an entire chapter of bean recipes, some as simple as mashing cooked lentils, forming into patties, and broiling like hamburgers.
- See Resources for highly recommended books on healthy cooking. And of course, *read this book* from cover to cover.

"I can't save money on groceries because I take my young children shopping with me, and I give in when they beg me for expensive treats."

- Don't give in! (Easier said than done.)
- Talk to your children before you go to the store. Explain that you will be buying only what is on your list.
- Let each child choose one inexpensive treat per visit ahead of time. Any whining or obnoxious behavior forfeits the treat.
- Go to the store at a time when everyone's rested and fed.
- Involve your young children in shopping, from fetching cans of corn to going through a pretend purse filled with "real stuff" just like Mommy uses at the store.
- Take along special toys to keep little hands occupied and attitudes cheerful.
- Play quiet games or read a book during a long wait in the checkout lane.
- Combine firm rules with a pleasant experience, so resistance is minimized the next time.
- Reward well-behaved children with genuine praise. A favorite activity, extra privilege, or piece of candy doesn't hurt, either.
- For older children and teens, schedule a trip to the supermarket as part of an afternoon outing that includes their favorite store. Christian knows, for example, that when it's his turn to help me grocery shop, I'll also take him to the football card shop.

"I can't save money on groceries because I do a lot of entertaining."

- Entertain with home-cooked meals whenever possible. Tablecloths, fresh flowers, candlelight, and delicious recipes make the simplest food seem elegant.
- Stick to cheap menus.
- Check out *More-with-Less Cookbook* from the library and read about Doris Janzen Longacre's "theme meals." Doris focuses on "one nutritious, cheap, but interesting dish," and adds a few simple, complimentary dishes. Her suggestions are intriguing and inexpensive.
- Limit hors d'oeuvres to cheaper varieties. Serve at tables rather than passing on trays.
- Host a potluck. You supply the main dish, dessert, drinks, and the house, and guests bring vegetables, salads, and/or breads.
- Choose an "off-time" for entertaining. Offer only snacks or desserts, or serve a brunch menu.
- Ask guests to B.Y.O.B. or other drinks.

"I can't save money on groceries because we're all big meat eaters, and meat is expensive."

- Dine on cheaper cuts of meat, like chicken. Buy whole chickens and Crock-Pot® them (so meat falls off the bones easily), or cut them into pieces yourself using a sharp knife and a standard cookbook's directions
- Buy a half or a quarter side of beef from the butcher or a local farmer and divide it up, if necessary, with friends.
- Make it a point to only buy meat that's on sale. Stock up when your favorites are cheapest, such as center-cut pork chops around Labor Day, turkeys at Thanksgiving, and hams in mid-December.
- Shop around for a supermarket that sells surplus, marked-down cuts. If your favorite supermarket doesn't do this, ask the meat manager if he'd consider it.
- Gradually decrease the portions of meat served in your meals, and supplement with more breads, grains, fruits, and vegetables.

"I can't save money on groceries because my family drinks cases of soda—and other expensive drinks—every week."

- Soda usually goes on sale just before Memorial Day, the Fourth of July, and Labor Day. Stock up then, and hide all those extra cases in an obscure corner of the garage.
- Gradually substitute other drinks. We used to serve Kool-Aid to the children every night for dinner and now we've converted to orange juice. Who says you have to serve juice for breakfast?
- See Chapter 3, "Make or Cook Your Own: Drinks," for ideas on lower-cost coffee.
- See Recipes for "homemade" drink ideas.
- Drink more water. If you can't stand the taste of tap water, try adding crushed ice and/or a slice of lemon. We have also found that water that stands in the refrigerator, open-topped, for a couple of days tastes better. (I read somewhere that some of the chlorine gas in the water evaporates.)

"I can't save money on groceries because my children will only eat expensive, highly processed foods."

- Give your children time to change. If kids get used to a steady diet of highly salted, sugary foods, their taste buds will need to gradually learn to like the relative blandness of good, everyday food.
- Introduce nutritious alternatives, one at a time, while gradually phasing out the junk. Find a healthy food, like grapes or bananas, that a child really likes, and serve it frequently.
- Begin to substitute raisins for candy, air-popped popcorn for potato chips, and homemade yogurt ice pops for candy bars.
- Remember that children go through phases. What they don't like today may become a favorite food tomorrow. Now and then, reintroduce small portions of new dishes.
- Serve your young child a little less food than you think he will eat; you can always dish out more later if he's hungry and has eaten it all. I've watched parents pile mountains of food on a child's plate, then constantly nag him to finish. To my mind, this is a totally unnecessary battle to have to fight.
- Involve your children in cooking. When we checked out a "Superheroes" cookbook from the library, Eric could hardly wait

to help prepare and eat some nutritious recipes. See Resources, *DC Super Heroes Super Healthy Cookbook*.

- Serve food in a way that's attractive to children. Jill Bond, author of *Mega-Cooking®*, sometimes arranges her children's salad in a sundae dish and calls her creation a "salad banana split." The banana is halved (as in a split) but is filled with scoops of chicken or potato salad. Salad dressing, cottage cheese, and additional fruit complete this masterpiece. Jill says she's never had a child turn one down.

- Use "props" to make good food more appealing. Young children who don't like milk may drink it from a special thermos or a "grown-up" glass with a special straw. Colorful plates and napkins help, too.

- Avoid food fights by giving children some choices. You can frame the question as, "Would you rather eat your peas or banana bread first?" instead of threatening, "If you don't eat those peas right now you're in time-out for an hour." I've been foolish enough to say something like this last remark, and know how poorly it works.

- Don't get into the habit of preparing whatever the child wants, especially if it's always different from the rest of the family's dinner. (There are exceptions to this, especially when you're dealing with a toddler on a temporary "food jag" who will only tolerate jelly sandwiches and applesauce.) Make a comment like, "I'm sorry you don't care for the chili, but this is what we're eating tonight. Would you like to help me prepare one of your favorite meals tomorrow night?"

- Offer no unhealthy alternatives. My children learned to drink water because, one summer, I simply told them that if they were thirsty between meals, they could have all the ice water they wanted. Period. Now they help themselves to the pitcher in the refrigerator several times a day.

- Make sure your children are genuinely hungry at mealtimes. When mine were still young enough to need two daily snacks, I tried to schedule them far enough away from lunch and dinner that they didn't interfere with young appetites. I remember that if Mary wasn't hungry at meals or snacks, we let her eat as little as she liked. But no dessert was offered, and she wasn't allowed to eat anything else until the next meal or snack.

- Read and talk about nutrition so your children understand why you're changing their eating habits. My little ones were fascinated by the lessons learned from *The Berenstain Bears and Too Much Junk Food*; soon afterward, Christian wanted "crunchy carrot sticks" every day, sometimes several times a day.

- Practice what you preach.

"I can't save money on groceries because I'm single and I eat out instead."

- Follow the basic guidelines that are outlined in Chapter 1, "Real-Life Shopping." Set a limit on spending, compare prices, buy most groceries from the cheapest store, supplement by shopping at other stores whose weekly specials are outstanding, make a detailed shopping list. Then . . .
- Pre-prepare several meals at once. For example, on a night when you're fixing spaghetti, triple the recipe. Eat your fill, then package the rest in meal-size portions. Freeze for later meals.
- Buy fresh vegetables and freeze them. Eileen Duggan, a single friend of mine who shared several of these suggestions, prefers fresh corn on the cob (in the husk), brussels sprouts, green beans, and mushrooms (freeze uncooked); she says they're delicious reheated from the freezer. Or buy frozen vegetables in large bags and cook only what you need for one meal.
- Take a simple, nutritious lunch, like a raw potato or half an acorn squash, to work for a quick fix in the microwave.
- Shop as infrequently as possible. Because she doesn't particularly like to shop, Eileen visits a farmers' market once a month for all her fruits and vegetables, Aldi once a month, and a discount supermarket if needed. She averages a total of a few hours, two to three shopping days each month. In this way, she spends little time buying food, has a well-stocked pantry on hand, and isn't as tempted to eat out.

"I can't save money on groceries because I can't be bothered with going to more than one grocery store."

- Go to one store, once a month, and do most of your shopping at a single time. Each week's grocery list should then be much smaller, making a quick weekly stop at your regular supermarket a manageable trip.
- "Beat the system" in that store. See Chapter 2.

- Try to buy only what's on sale, especially loss leaders, and stock up when you can.
- Purchase generic or store brand goods rather than name brand products.
- Ask the store meat manager about marked-down cuts of meat, and deli meat and cheese "ends." A friendly butcher can also offer good advice on bargain meats and ways to tenderize and cook them. Buy family pack quantities, or ask the meat manager directly about purchasing 10-pounds-plus packages.
- Talk to the store produce manager about selling slightly damaged or bruised fruits and vegetables at half price.
- Have your friends and relatives call both the store meat manager and produce manager with the same requests. If enough people ask for discounted foods, supermarkets will usually try to oblige.
- Clip coupons religiously. Visit the store on double coupon days.
- Buy all your meat for the month one week when sales are particularly good, all your canned and long-term supplies the next week, all your freezeable breads the next, most of your produce the next . . . you get the idea.

"I can't save money on groceries because I eat only high-priced natural, organic, whole foods."

- Then buy whole and natural foods through a co-op rather than a health food store. If there is currently no co-op in your area, contact the nearest food warehouse for information on how to organize one. See Resources, "U.S. Cooperative Food Warehouses."
- Learn to cook most of your food from scratch, using wholesome ingredients you can control.
- Purchase meat directly from farmers you know and trust.
- Grow your own. Your Cooperative Extension Service agent will be glad to provide materials that show you how to garden organically.
- Process your own food through canning, freezing, drying, and pickling.
- Set up an informal cooperative with other friends, and take turns buying in bulk from produce wholesalers. You can scout out organic growers ahead of time.
- Buy from farmers' markets. Jill Bond, author of *Mega-Cooking*, says she has found small farmers at these markets who sell produce that's grown organically. From Jill's experience, the fruits and vegetables don't always cost extra.
- Call a local bartering exchange to find out if joining an exchange

might enable you to trade with an organic foods supplier. See Resources, "Organizations and More."

"I can't save money on groceries because I have teenagers who eat me out of house and home."

- Decide ahead of time what you'll make available for snacks and impromptu meals, and post it on the refrigerator. If your teen eats what isn't on the "Okay to Eat" list, he pays for it, suggests Pat Edwards, author of *Cheap Eating*.
- Keep sugary and/or junk foods out of the house. Instead, make sure there are plenty of nutritious foods—fresh fruits, veggies and dip, etc.—on hand.
- Have snacks waiting near the door or on the table when your teen walks into the kitchen. Everything should be already washed, diced, sliced, or otherwise prepared and ready to eat. The trick is to get him interested in what's convenient, rather than raiding the refrigerator and pantry, when he's starved.
- For meals, serve plenty of beans, whole grains, rice, pasta, casseroles, and soups—foods that are filling and healthful. One mother told me she buys 25-pound bags of whole-wheat flour, and always tries to have homemade breads, muffins, waffles, and pancakes available for hungry young people.
- Involve your teenagers in gardening. They'll be more likely to eat produce when they've helped raise it. (A mother of thirteen suggested this, and I'll bet their garden was monstrous.)
- Keep a big pot of stew or chili simmering in the Crock-Pot slow cooker all weekend, says Mike Yorkey, author of *Saving Money Any Way You Can,* so in-and-out-the-door families always have an instant meal ready.
- Encourage your teens to help with shopping and cooking. Shopping gives them an idea of the cost of food, and also a chance to buy more expensive, favorite items with their own money if those particular foods are not in your budget. Cooking helps ensure that there are foods around the house that teens especially like. Then, in answer to the complaint "There's nothing to eat here that I like," you can reply sweetly, "I have all the ingredients on hand for you to make your favorite banana bread."
- Mega-cook or try once-a-month cooking, so there are foods in your freezer available for snacks and quick meals. This can be as painless as simply assembling several pizzas the next time you make one, then freezing the extras.

"I can't save money on groceries because I end up buying so many extra treats for birthdays and holidays."

- Set a budget for birthdays and holidays and stick to it.
- Use your creativity—rather than your pocketbook—to make celebrations special. For each of our children's birthdays, we make cut-up cakes from a plain sheet cake sliced into interesting shapes, frosted, and decorated. It's been fun, through the years, to see the results: a butterfly, baby booties, Raggedy Ann, even cakes that were carved to look like a grand piano and landscaped like a golf course!
- Stock up on food for birthday parties by purchasing ice cream, soda, and other treats on sale—using double coupons, if possible. Plan ahead.
- Bulk buy candy as party favors. Package it yourself.
- Understand, when dealing with children, that giving them everything money can buy is fulfilling a want, not a need.
- Compromise. Offer alternatives, such as a sleepover with VCR movies and homemade caramel corn, instead of a pizza party for twenty. Is your child willing to finance an expensive party from his own savings?
- Give homemade gifts of food at Christmastime. Modify the recipes to make them healthier. Or assemble dry soup mixes with recipes attached. Bake whole-grain breads and muffins. Share coupons for complete, to-be-delivered dinners.

"I can't save money on groceries because I don't see any need to do so."

- Then calculate how much you're spending on food right now. If your current weekly average is $150, and you cut back to $100, that's more than a $200 monthly savings, or $2,600 a year. (You can also think of it as $2,600 of tax-free income.) Is there anything else on which you would rather be spending this money?

"I can't save money on groceries because I just plain don't want to."

- Then . . . well, sorry. I don't have an answer for that one!

CHAPTER 6

Healthy, Low-Cost Recipes

My purpose in including this chapter on recipes is certainly not to try to impress you with my culinary skills. Compared to my mother and mother-in-law, I'm afraid I'm not much of a cook. Still, I could imagine someone writing, after reading the text, and saying something like, "You can't really make a yeast bread in 90 minutes total, can you? How do you do that?" The recipes are here to prove that low-cost, healthy eating is not only possible but also delicious.

The first section, "Meats and Main Dishes," includes mostly inexpensive entrees. "Breads and Breakfast Foods" features some of our favorite recipes. "Side Dishes" explains how to prepare vegetables, salads, and fruits; "Miscellaneous," additional foods plus drinks. "Desserts" includes a variety of sweet treats that, used sparingly, will enrich your family's meals.

Most of the recipes in this chapter are ones that I personally prepare. But for variety's sake, I've also added some that reflect other families' styles of cooking as well as their opinions of what healthy eating means. JoAnna Lund's desserts, for example, are all no-sugar (she uses artificial sweeteners), low-sodium, low-fat recipes. I've also included desserts that use sugar in moderation, and some that use honey. Take your pick, according to your personal definition of what's good for you.

Remember the Introduction, where I told you that "the experts" can disagree? Readers will, too, so I'm offering a variety of choices. You can alternate low-fat, low-calorie, and low-sugar dishes with richer desserts and side dishes. Serve a dinner that's high in protein one night, and the next, a vegetarian soup. There are all sorts of choices in this chapter.

At any rate, here are several recipes that have been helpful to me as I've learned to serve my family healthy foods for $12 a day.

MEATS AND MAIN DISHES

Baked Fruity Chicken

Serves 6

Adapted from a recipe in *The $30 a Week Grocery Budget, Volume I,* by Donna McKenna.

Preheat oven to 350 degrees. Coat a 9-x-13-inch pan with nonstick baking spray. Place in the pan:

2 to 2½ pounds chicken pieces

Flip the pieces so both sides are coated. Top with:

Marmalade, preserves or jelly, enough to lightly cover all chicken pieces

Bake for 45 to 50 minutes.

Variations: Sprinkle with any combination of salt, pepper, oregano, basil, rosemary, poultry seasoning, or paprika. Or pour tomato sauce over all the chicken pieces.

Tips: Donna recommends removing the chicken from the pan about 15 minutes before the meat is done, then filling the pan with a layer of cooked rice or cooked, cut-up potatoes. Place the chicken back on top and bake another 15 minutes. We've tried this and it's delicious.

Nutritional Data for One Serving (about 5 to 6 ounces): Calories: 367, Calories from Fat: 181, Total Fat: 20 g, Saturated Fat: 6 g, Cholesterol: 162 mg, Sodium: 120 mg, Total Carbohydrate: 3 g, Dietary Fiber: 0 g, Sugars: 0 g, Protein: 41 g, Vitamin A: 29% RDA, Vitamin C: 2% RDA, Calcium: 2% RDA, Iron: 14% RDA

Beef and Noodle Soup

From *Healthy Exchanges Food Newsletter.**

1 full cup diced cooked lean roast beef (6 ounces)
½ cup chopped onion
1 ¾ cups canned beef broth (14½-ounce can)
2 ¼ cups water
⅛ teaspoon black pepper
¼ teaspoon minced garlic
1 ¾ cups uncooked noodles (3 ounces)
½ cup canned mushrooms, drained (2½-ounce jar)
1 teaspoon dried parsley flakes

In a large saucepan sprayed with butter-flavored cooking spray, sauté diced roast beef and onion. Add beef broth, water, black pepper, and minced garlic. Bring mixture to a boil. Reduce heat. Simmer 10 minutes. Add noodles, mushrooms, and parsley flakes. Cover. Cook 10 minutes longer or until noodles are tender. Freezes well.

Serves 4 (1½ cups)
Each serving equals:
HE: 1 ½ Protein, 1 Bread, ½ Vegetable, 9 Optional Calories
205 Calories, 5 gm Fat, 17 gm Protein, 23 gm Carbohydrate, 492 mg Sodium, 3 gm Fiber
Diabetic: 1 ½ Meat, 1 ½ Starch

HINT: Purchase a chunk of roast beef from your local deli or a pkg of Healthy Choice sliced luncheon meats and dice either when you get home.

*Note: The format of this recipe differs from most recipes in this book at JoAnna Lund's—the author's—request that her original recipe remain exactly as it appeared in her newsletter.

Broiled Halibut in Soy Sauce

Serves 4 to 6

Place in an ungreased 9-x-13-inch baking pan:

1 to 1½ pounds halibut steaks

Mix together:
   ¼ cup water
   3 tablespoons lemon juice
   2 tablespoons soy sauce
   1 teaspoon ginger
   ¾ teaspoon grated lemon peel
   ½ teaspoon minced garlic

Pour liquid over fish. Cover and refrigerate for several hours. When ready to eat, preheat oven to broil. Drain fish, reserving liquid. Place fish on rack sprayed with nonstick cooking spray. Lightly coat fish with reserved liquid. Broil 5 to 7 minutes on each side, occasionally coating with extra liquid.

Variations: This recipe is delicious with other varieties of fish. Try it with your latest catch.

Tips: Fish does not have to be marinated in advance if you're in a hurry, but marinade does improve flavor.

Nutritional Data for One Serving (about 4 ounces): Calories: 159, Calories from Fat: 30, Total Fat: 3 g, Saturated Fat: 0 g, Cholesterol: 43 mg, Sodium: 487 mg, Total Carbohydrate: 2 g, Dietary Fiber: 0 g, Sugars: 0 g, Protein: 29 g, Vitamin A: 6% RDA, Vitamin C: 5% RDA, Calcium: 7% RDA, Iron: 7% RDA

Cabbage Rolls

Serves 4 to 6

Adapted from the recipe of my German friend, Anneliese Thomas.

Thoroughly wash:

1 medium-size head green cabbage

Remove brown or damaged leaves. Cut 1 inch off the bottom of the cabbage and discard. Fill a large pan with:

2 cups water

Bring to a boil. Cook cabbage about 15 minutes, until leaves separate. Drain cabbage in colander. Cool. In the meantime, brown in a large frying pan:

6 ounces very lean ground beef or ground turkey
1 medium onion, chopped finely
2 cloves garlic, minced

Drain fat. Add:

1 cup tomato sauce
1 28-ounce can tomatoes
Salt and pepper to taste

Stir occasionally, and cook until onions are tender. Set aside. Pull 10 large outer leaves from cabbage and set aside. Dice remaining cabbage into small shreds and add to meat mixture. Preheat oven to 375 degrees. Coat a shallow 9-x-13-inch baking pan with nonstick cooking spray.

Spread out large cabbage leaves on the counter. Using a slotted spoon to dish up meat (and thus drain it somewhat), fill each leaf with about ⅓ cup meat mixture. Fold right and left sides of the leaves toward the middle, then roll from near to far. Secure each leaf with a toothpick.

Place cabbage rolls in baking dish. Pour remaining sauce over rolls.

Cover with foil. Bake in preheated oven about 1 hour, or until cabbage is tender.

Variations: Make a gravy rather than tomato sauce; see Recipe Index.

Tips: Be sure you cook the cabbage until it's very tender. I once made the mistake of shortening the boiling time: my cabbage was nearly raw, even after a long time in the oven. Add extra seasonings if you're cooking with ground turkey.

Nutritional Data for One Serving (2 rolls): Calories: 173, Calories from Fat: 61, Total Fat: 7 g, Saturated Fat: 2 g, Cholesterol: 23 mg, Sodium: 936 mg, Total Carbohydrate: 20 g, Dietary Fiber: 7 g, Sugars: 12 g, Protein: 12 g, Vitamin A: 12% RDA, Vitamin C: 222% RDA, Calcium: 15% RDA, Iron: 14% RDA

Cheesy Tuna Garden Skillet

From *Healthy Exchanges Food Newsletter**

1 (6-ounce) can white albacore tuna, packed in water, drained and flaked
1 (10¾-ounce) can Campbell's Healthy Request Cream of Mushroom soup
⅓ cup skim milk
¾ cup shredded Kraft reduced-fat cheddar cheese (3 ounces)
¼ cup grated Kraft House Italian or Parmesan cheese (¾ ounce)
1 teaspoon dried parsley flakes
¼ teaspoon black pepper
2 cups canned sliced carrots, rinsed and drained (16-ounce can)
2 cups canned French-style green beans, rinsed and drained (16-ounce can)
2 cups cooked noodles

In a large skillet, combine tuna, mushroom soup, and skim milk. Stir in cheddar cheese, House Italian cheese, parsley flakes, and black pepper. Mix well to combine. Cook over medium heat, stirring often, until cheese melts. Add carrots and green beans. Mix well to combine. Stir in noodles. Continue cooking, stirring often, until mixture is heated through. Freezes well.

Serves 6 (1 cup)
Each serving equals:
HE: 1 ⅓ Protein, 1⅓ Vegetable, ⅔ Bread, ¼ Slider, 13 Optional Calories
209 Calories, 5 gm Fat, 17 gm Protein, 24 gm Carbohydrate, 505 mg Sodium, 3 gm Fiber
Diabetic: 1½ Meat, 1½ Vegetable, 1 Starch

HINT: A full 1¾ cups dry noodles usually makes about 2 cups cooked.

*Note: The format of this recipe differs from most others in this book at JoAnna Lund's—the author's—request that her original recipe remain exactly as it appeared in her newsletter.

Chicken, Bean, and Noodle Soup

Serves as many as you need to serve

Combine in a Crock-Pot slow cooker:

All the leftover vegetables in your refrigerator that are less than four days old and/or smell okay and look okay, chopped into bite-size pieces
Any bits of meat or vegetables stored in the "soup bowl" in your freezer
Leftover pasta
Dabs of beans
Defatted meat broth or 3 to 4 bouillon cubes
Salt, pepper, garlic, and onion to taste
Enough water to cover it all

Cook 8 to 10 hours on low.

Variations: Instead of using a slow cooker, simmer your soup on the stove until vegetables are tender.

Tips: My last soup—a very successful one—combined bits of cooked chicken, a few tablespoons of baked beans, some whole-wheat noodles, and a little broccoli and corn. See, you *can* use up leftovers.

Nutritional Data: Sorry, there's no way a nutritionist could analyze this one. Rest assured that if you keep the amount of meat small and use defatted broth, you'll have a healthy, delicious entree.

Chicken in Barbecue Sauce

Serves 6 to 8

Preheat oven to 350 degrees. Mix barbecue sauce in a saucepan:

½ cup chopped onion
½ cup ketchup
⅓ cup honey
2 teaspoons Worcestershire sauce
Dash of pepper

Cook over low heat for 3 minutes. Set aside. Coat the bottom of a nonstick frying pan with nonstick cooking spray. On medium-high heat, quickly brown:

2 to 3 pounds cut-up chicken pieces

Coat large casserole dish with nonstick cooking spray. Place seared chicken in dish. Cover with generous amounts of barbecue sauce. Bake for about 1 hour, or until tender.

Variations: Use barbecue sauce on pork, beef, turkey, or any other meat that happens to be on sale for the week.

Tips: Cook vegetables in the oven along with the meat, preferably in a layer below it in the same pan.

Nutritional Data for One Serving (5 to 6 ounces): Calories: 372, Calories from Fat: 159, Total Fat: 18 g, Saturated Fat: 5 g, Cholesterol: 137 mg, Sodium: 309 mg, Total Carbohydrate: 17 g, Dietary Fiber: 0 g, Sugars: 2 g, Protein: 35 g, Vitamin A: 26% RDA, Vitamin C: 11% RDA, Calcium: 3% RDA, Iron: 14% RDA

Chili

Serves 6 to 8

Combine in a large metal saucepan:

2 15-ounce cans red beans, liquid included
1 15-ounce can kidney beans, liquid included
1 large onion, finely chopped
1 green pepper, finely chopped
¼ cup molasses
2 teaspoons salt
Chili powder to taste
Garlic powder to taste

Simmer for 1 to 2 hours, until flavors are well blended. Serve topped with low-fat cheese and/or croutons.

Variations: Add leftover (lean) cooked meat of your choice. Discard liquid from beans and substitute one large can tomato or vegetable juice. Use canned tomatoes and extra seasoning in place of bean liquid. Substitute dry beans in place of canned beans for a better value; see package for cooking directions.

Tips: Cook in a Crock-Pot slow cooker for 8 hours or more; flavor improves with longer simmering time.

Nutritional Data for One Serving (about 1 cup): Calories: 206, Calories from Fat: 8, Total Fat: 1 g, Saturated Fat: 0 g, Cholesterol: 0 mg, Sodium: 1,241 mg, Total Carbohydrate: 40 g, Dietary Fiber: 10 g, Sugars: 4 g, Protein: 11 g, Vitamin A: 6% RDA, Vitamin C: 59% RDA, Calcium: 15% RDA, Iron: 29% RDA

Enchilada Bake

Serves 6

Adapted from a recipe by Jan Kent, author of
the *A Taste of Dutch* cookbook.

Preheat oven to 350 degrees. Brown in a frying pan:

½ pound very lean ground beef or lean ground turkey
1 onion, finely chopped
1 carrot, grated
1 green or yellow pepper, finely chopped

Add to the above mixture:

1 large can Brooks Chili Hot Beans, drained
1 15-ounce can tomato sauce

Cook until bubbly. Meanwhile, grate:

2 cups low-fat mozzarella cheese

Set aside. Open and set aside:

1 package of 8 corn tortillas

Coat a 9-x-13-inch baking pan with nonstick cooking spray. Layer
sauce mixture, mozzarella cheese, corn tortilla. Repeat until ingredients are all layered. Bake for 20 minutes, until heated through.

Variations: Replace meat mixture with all beans. Use dried beans—
instead of canned—and increase amounts of seasonings used.

Tips: Substitute store-bought taco seasoning mix for my recipe
below.

Nutritional Data for One Serving (about 1¼ cups): Calories: 430, Calories from Fat: 147,
Total Fat: 16 g, Saturated Fat: 7 g, Cholesterol: 47 mg, Sodium: 1,285 mg, Total Carbohydrate: 54 g,
Dietary Fiber: 5 g, Sugars: 2 g, Protein: 27 g, Vitamin A: 60% RDA, Vitamin C: 75% RDA, Calcium: 40%
RDA, Iron: 26% RDA

Taco Seasoning Mix

Combine:

> **2 teaspoons chili powder**
> **2 teaspoons dried parsley flakes**
> **1½ teaspoons cumin**
> **1 teaspoon paprika**
> **1 teaspoon onion salt**
> **½ teaspoon oregano**
> **½ teaspoon garlic powder**

This recipe is equivalent to a 1¼-ounce package of store-bought seasoning mix, and cheaper, especially if you buy spices in bulk and/or at a discount.

Enchiladas with Chicken

Serves 6

Dice:

> **3 cups cooked chicken**

Place in nonstick frying pan. Add:

> **1 cup water**
> **1 package taco seasoning mix**

Set aside. Shred:

> **6 cups lettuce**

Place in large bowl. Set aside. Grate:

> **6 ounces part-skim mozzarella (or other favorite low-fat) cheese**

Place in a bowl. Set aside. Dice:

1 large tomato

Heat:

1 12-count package of flour or corn tortillas

In the oven or microwave according to package directions. Assemble on tortillas: cheese, hot meat mixture, lettuce, tomatoes. Fold bottom one-fourth of tortilla horizontally toward the top. Roll rest of tortilla vertically into a cylinder. Secure with toothpicks.

Variations: We usually assemble these enchiladas one at a time at the table. But sometimes I prepare several in advance, line them in a cake pan coated with nonstick cooking spray, spread a thin row of salsa and low-fat cheese on top, and bake for 10 minutes in a 400-degree oven. Any meat or bean mixture will substitute for chicken, but more seasoning is required for dried beans. I sometimes add leftover vegetables. Make your own taco seasoning mix, listed above.

Tips: Tortillas can be made by hand, but the process takes time. For a very similar taste, fry the store-bought version in a tiny bit of olive oil.

Nutritional Data for One Serving (2 enchiladas): Calories: 462, Calories from Fat: 151, Total Fat: 17 g, Saturated Fat: 6 g, Cholesterol: 81 mg, Sodium: 891 mg, Total Carbohydrate: 43 g, Dietary Fiber: 1 g, Sugars: 2 g, Protein: 33 g, Vitamin A: 15% RDA, Vitamin C: 12% RDA, Calcium: 31% RDA, Iron: 24% RDA

Frankfurter Special

Serves 6

Preheat broiler. Combine in a saucepan:

1 tart medium apple, cored and diced
1 15-ounce can chunky pineapple
1 cup canned carrots
¼ cup water
1 chicken bouillon cube
1 tablespoon tomato juice
1 tablespoon lemon juice
½ tablespoon cider vinegar
⅛ teaspoon ginger

Place pan on burner over low heat. In the meantime, slice lengthwise, but not completely in two:

12 turkey or chicken hot dogs

Place in broiler and cook until hot dogs are heated through, about 3 minutes per side. While hot dogs are cooking, begin stirring liquid mixture, stirring frequently for about 10 minutes. Add broiled hot dogs and cook another 3 minutes.

Variations: The original recipe called for ⅛ teaspoon cayenne pepper and ½ tablespoon curry powder added to the recipe above. Use fresh, diced carrots in place of cooked carrots.

Tips: For smaller children, you may want to cut the hot dogs into tiny pieces before adding them to the liquid.

Nutritional Data for One Serving (2 hot dogs with sauce): Calories: 268, Calories from Fat: 146, Total Fat: 16 g, Saturated Fat: 5 g, Cholesterol: 96 mg, Sodium: 1,353 mg, Total Carbohydrate: 18 g, Dietary Fiber: 1 g, Sugars: 15 g, Protein: 14 g, Vitamin A: 34% RDA, Vitamin C: 16% RDA, Calcium: 11% RDA, Iron: 12% RDA

"Fried" Chicken

Serves 6

Preheat oven to 400 degrees. Line a 9-x-13-inch pan with foil, then place a wire rack on top. Coat the rack with nonstick cooking spray. Cut up:

1 3-to-4-pound fryer (or 3 to 4 pounds of cut-up chicken)

Wash chicken thoroughly with cold water. Pat dry. Set aside. In a small plastic bag, combine:

1 cup whole-wheat bread crumbs, finely crumbled
¾ teaspoon onion powder
¾ teaspoon paprika
¾ teaspoon celery salt

Set aside. Brush chicken pieces with:

¼ cup plain nonfat yogurt

Shake the "spice bag" thoroughly, then dip chicken pieces, one at a time, into the bag. Place pieces on rack so they do not touch. Bake 45 to 50 minutes, until chicken is lightly browned and juices run clear when pierced with a fork.

Variations: Substitute cracker crumbs or cornflake crumbs for bread crumbs. Use any spice combination you like (no need to panic if you're out of celery salt).
Tips: Don't overcook the chicken or it becomes tough. Decide when it's finished by the fork test rather than the color test.

Nutritional Data for One Serving (about 8 ounces): Calories: 470, Calories from Fat: 163, Total Fat: 18 g, Saturated Fat: 10 g, Cholesterol: 232 mg, Sodium: 718 mg, Total Carbohydrate: 14 g, Dietary Fiber: 0 g, Sugars: 0 g, Protein: 62 g, Vitamin A: 2% RDA, Vitamin C: 1% RDA, Calcium: 14% RDA, Iron: 48% RDA

Hamburger Stroganoff

Serves 6

Adapted from a recipe in *The $30 a Week Grocery Budget, Volume I.*

Place a little water in a large frying pan. Sauté:

1 medium onion, finely chopped
1 clove garlic, crushed

Cook until limp. Add:

8 ounces cooked lean hamburger
1½ cups water
5 beef bouillon cubes
Salt and pepper to taste

Cover and cook. Meanwhile, place in a plastic container:

1½ tablespoons cornstarch
½ cup water

Cover with a tight-fitting lid. Shake vigorously until cornstarch is dissolved in liquid. Bring meat mixture to a boil. Add cornstarch-and-water mixture, stirring constantly until meat mixture boils again. Boil and stir for 1 more minute. Remove from heat. Add:

1 cup plain nonfat yogurt

Stir thoroughly. Serve over brown rice or whole-wheat noodles.

Variations: Use whatever precooked meat you have on hand; the original recipe calls for hamburger. Add a can of (drained) mushrooms to the above ingredients.

Tips: You can substitute a can of cream of mushroom soup for the cornstarch-and-water mixture, but remember this drives up both the fat content and the cost.

Nutritional Data for One Serving (about 1 cup meat and gravy): Calories: 131, Calories from Fat: 34, Total Fat: 4 g, Saturated Fat: 1 g, Cholesterol: 37 mg, Sodium: 229 mg, Total Carbohydrate: 7 g, Dietary Fiber: 1 g, Sugars: 3 g, Protein: 16 g, Vitamin A: 0% RDA, Vitamin C: 4% RDA, Calcium: 9% RDA, Iron: 8% RDA

Haystacks

Sorvos as many as you like

Adapted from a recipe by Jan Kent, author
of *A Taste of Dutch* cookbook.

"Stack" the following ingredients on each person's plate:

Crushed corn tortillas or reduced-fat corn chips
Cooked brown rice
Red chili beans (from a can or cooked dried beans)
Grated low-fat cheese
Chopped lettuce or greens
Chopped tomatoes
Diced onions
A few black olives

Top with:

Taco sauce or salsa
Nonfat Ranch dressing

Variations: This dish couldn't be more versatile, could it?

Tips: If using dried beans, be sure to start preparing them the night before you serve Haystacks. See Basic Beans in Recipe Index.

Nutritional Data for One Serving: Too hard to figure.

Hazel's Five-Hour Stew

Serves 4 to 6

Adapted from a recipe from my friend, Carol Haynes.

Preheat oven to 250 degrees. Place in a large, ovenproof casserole dish:

3 cups diced, uncooked chicken
6 carrots, sliced
2 medium onions, diced
½ cup celery, sliced
1 small can peas, drained
1 12-ounce can tomato juice
¾ cup tomato paste
¼ cup water
1½ teaspoons salt
1 teaspoon sugar
½ teaspoon pepper

Mix thoroughly. Cover casserole dish with a lid. Bake for 5 hours.

Variations: Simmer this stew in a Crock-Pot slow cooker, instead of in the oven, for 8 to 10 hours on low setting.

Tips: The original recipe calls for uncooked beef stew meat instead of chicken; by substituting chicken, you may find the stew too bland for your tastes. Sample it first, and add extra seasonings as needed.

Nutritional Data for One Serving (a big bowl): Calories: 295, Calories from Fat: 75, Total Fat: 8 g, Saturated Fat: 2 g, Cholesterol: 74 mg, Sodium: 1,345 mg, Total Carbohydrate: 29 g, Dietary Fiber: 7 g, Sugars: 12 g, Protein: 27 g, Vitamin A: 260% RDA, Vitamin C: 70% RDA, Calcium: 8% RDA, Iron: 20% RDA

Italian Chicken and Angel Hair Pasta

Serves 6 to 8

Prepare according to package directions:

16 ounces angel hair pasta

Set aside. Melt over medium heat in a large frying pan:

2 tablespoons butter or margarine

Add:

1 pound raw chicken, cut into bite-size pieces
1 small onion, diced
1 clove garlic, minced

Cook and stir until tender. Add a little water if needed. Drain. Stir in:

4 8-ounce cans tomato sauce
1 16-ounce can tomatoes
1 tablespoon Worcestershire or soy sauce
2 tablespoons Italian seasoning

Simmer, covered, stirring occasionally, for 10 to 15 minutes. Serve hot over pasta.

Variations: Any pasta will do; buy what's on sale. You can purchase spaghetti sauce in a jar instead of making your own from tomatoes, sauce, Worcestershire, and Italian seasoning.

Tips: To lower fat and calories even more, eliminate margarine and sauté chicken, onion, and garlic in a small amount of water. Or used reduced-fat margarine.

Nutritional Data for One Serving (a big plateful): Calories: 454, Calories from Fat: 95, Total Fat: 11g, Saturated Fat: 2 g, Cholesterol: 57 mg, Sodium: 1,002 mg, Total Carbohydrate: 63 g, Dietary Fiber: 2 g, Sugars: 4 g, Protein: 28 g, Vitamin A: 23% RDA, Vitamin C: 38% RDA, Calcium: 8% RDA, Iron: 31% RDA

Lasagna

Serves 14 to 16

Preheat oven to 400 degrees. Brown in a large frying pan:

1 pound extra-lean ground beef or ground turkey
1 large onion, chopped finely

Add and simmer for 1 hour:

2 15-ounce cans tomatoes
3 8-ounce cans tomato sauce
2 tablespoons sugar
1 tablespoon Worcestershire sauce
2 tablespoons Italian seasoning

Meanwhile, in a separate bowl, combine:

1 pound small-curd, low-fat cottage cheese
6 egg whites
½ cup Parmesan cheese

Prepare according to package directions:

1 16-ounce package lasagna noodles

Set aside. Grate and set aside:

1 pound mozzarella cheese

Coat two large 9-x-13-inch cake pans with nonstick cooking spray. Layer cooked noodles, cottage cheese mixture, mozzarella cheese, and meat/tomato sauce, first in one pan, then the other. Bake for 45 minutes. Let stand for 10 minutes before serving.

Variations: Substitute your favorite spaghetti sauce for the tomato sauce mixture. Skip cooking the noodles, but make sure dry noodles are thoroughly covered with sauce; add a little extra water, then bake the dish at a slightly lower temperature and a little longer than usual.

Tips: This recipe is expensive to make but produces quite a lot of a very filling entree. It freezes well and actually improves in flavor after a day in the refrigerator. I often add more diced vegetables and decrease the amount of meat. (By the way, this is the same sauce from the previous recipe, Italian Chicken and Angel Hair Pasta.)

Nutritional Data for One Serving (about 1 4-inch square): Calories: 345, Calories from Fat: 116, Total Fat: 13 g, Saturated Fat: 6 g, Cholesterol: 70 mg, Sodium: 751 mg, Total Carbohydrate: 32 g, Dietary Fiber: 1 g, Sugars: 5 g, Protein: 25 g, Vitamin A: 15% RDA, Vitamin C: 23% RDA, Calcium: 30% RDA, Iron: 10% RDA

Minestrone

Serves 4 to 6

Adapted from a recipe in *Cheap Eating*, by Pat Edwards.

Dice into bite-size pieces:

2 carrots
1 large onion
1 large potato

Set aside. Pour into large frying pan:

3 tablespoons canola oil

Heat. Add diced vegetables and sauté. Add:

1 can crushed tomatoes
5 cups water
Rind of Parmesan cheese (or 2 ounces Parmesan cheese)

Let simmer for 1 hour.

Variations: Substitute 1 tablespoon tomato paste for the can of crushed tomatoes.
Tips: Cook this in your slow cooker instead of on the stove.

Nutritional Data for One Serving (1 bowl): Calories: 243, Calories from Fat: 105, Total Fat: 12 g, Saturated Fat: 1 g, Cholesterol: 8 mg, Sodium: 402 mg, Total Carbohydrate: 29 g, Dietary Fiber: 3 g, Sugars: 5 g, Protein: 8 g, Vitamin A: 93% RDA, Vitamin C: 65% RDA, Calcium: 19% RDA, Iron: 11% RDA

Momwiches

Serves 6 to 8

Adapted from a recipe in *A Taste of Dutch,* a cookbook by Jan Kent.

Brown in a large frying pan:

1 pound very lean ground beef or ground turkey

Sauté in a separate pan:

1 onion, diced
½ cup green pepper, diced
½ cup celery, diced
Enough water to just cover the bottom of the pan

Drain any grease from meat. Add diced vegetables. Also add:

1 cup ketchup
¼ cup vinegar
¼ cup brown sugar
1 teaspoon chili powder
½ teaspoon salt
½ teaspoon paprika
⅛ teaspoon pepper

Cover and simmer for 20 to 30 minutes. Serve on whole-wheat buns or bread.

Variations: You can simplify this recipe considerably by eliminating most of the vegetables and spices (though the taste won't be the same, of course).

Tips: This recipe's taste is very similar to that of Manwich sloppy joes, only much cheaper.

Nutritional Data for One Serving (1 generous sandwich, with meat left over) Calories: 239, Calories from Fat: 102, Total Fat: 11 g, Saturated Fat: 4 g, Cholesterol: 43 mg, Sodium: 679 mg, Total Carbohydrate: 23 g, Dietary Fiber: 2 g, Sugars: 6 g, Protein: 13 g, Vitamin A: 7% RDA, Vitamin C: 39% RDA, Calcium: 3% RDA, Iron: 11% RDA

O'Brion's Irish Dish

Serves 8

Adapted from a recipe in *The $30 a Week Grocery Budget,
Volume II,* by Donna McKenna.

Preheat oven to 350 degrees. Cook in a frying pan over medium heat:

**3 cups chicken, cut into bite-size pieces
½ cup defatted ham broth**

Cook until chicken is tender, stirring occasionally. Set aside. Dice into bite-size pieces:

**6 large potatoes, peeled
1 large onion
1 large green pepper**

Coat a 9-x-13-inch baking pan with nonstick cooking spray. Mix chicken and vegetables, and place in pan. Bake for 40 to 45 minutes, until vegetables break easily with a fork.

Variations: The original recipe called for 1 package of Italian sausage. I discovered—by accident—that chicken cooked in ham broth tastes somewhat like sausage. But you can use whatever meat and/or broth you have on hand.

Tips: Add half a package of onion soup mix if you'd like a more seasoned taste.

Nutritional Data for One Serving (a large plateful): Calories: 260, Calories from Fat: 45, Total Fat: 5 g, Saturated Fat: 1 g, Cholesterol: 46 mg, Sodium: 100 mg, Total Carbohydrate: 36 g, Dietary Fiber: 4 g, Sugars: 1 g, Protein: 18 g, Vitamin A: 3% RDA, Vitamin C: 101% RDA, Calcium: 3% RDA, Iron: 13% RDA

One-Dish Meal

Serves as many as you like

Here's another of those totally flexible dishes that work especially well with leftovers. Choose one item or a combination of items from each of the four categories below.

1. **1½ cups vegetables: mixed vegetables, tomatoes, corn, green beans, broccoli, peas, cabbage, and/or cooked and cubed acorn squash, zucchini, or potatoes**
2. **1½ to 2 cups chicken, fish, eggs, meat, dried beans or peas; canned tuna or other meat; cooked meat, such as hamburger, turkey, chicken, pork, or lean sausage; hard-cooked egg; and/or cooked lentils, split peas, navy beans, or pinto beans**
3. **1 to 1½ cups liquid ingredients: cheese or white sauce; cream soup, such as mushroom, chicken, celery, or broccoli; cheese soup; evaporated milk; tomato soup or sauce; or shredded cheese plus milk**
4. **1 to 1½ cups bread, rice, or pasta; cubed bread and/or cooked macaroni, noodles, rice, spaghetti, barley, or bulgur**

Preheat oven to 325 degrees. Lightly coat a casserole dish with non-stick cooking spray. Combine all choices of ingredients in a large bowl. Add appropriate seasonings, such as sautéed garlic and/or onion, salt, pepper, paprika, etc. Mix thoroughly. Place in casserole dish. If desired, add toppings such as bread crumbs, cracker crumbs, or grated Parmesan cheese. Bake, covered, for 30 minutes. Bake 15 minutes longer to brown topping.

Variations: Place ingredients in large skillet. Simmer, uncovered, on top of stove until bubbly.

Tips: Be sure the leftovers you use in this dish aren't spoiled: perishable leftovers in the refrigerator keep no longer than four days at most, and leftover gravy and broth, no longer than two days. (If you store them in the freezer, your "safe" period extends to three months.)

Nutritional Data for One Serving: That really depends on what you put into this casserole.

Pizza

Serves 6

Combine in a small bowl:

1 cup very hot water
2 teaspoons yeast (or 2 packages)

Mix thoroughly and set aside. In a larger bowl, combine.

2½ cups white flour
1½ cups whole-wheat flour
1½ teaspoons salt
3 tablespoons honey
2 tablespoons canola or olive oil
2 egg whites

Add yeast mixture to flour mixture. Stir together until completely blended. Knead by hand for 2 minutes, adding flour as needed. Cover bowl with a clean dishcloth and set in a warm place. Let rise until doubled in size, about 2 to 3 hours.

Divide dough into two mounds. Add enough flour to take the stickiness out of each mound, working flour into each mound. One at a time, on a floured surface, roll out dough to desired thickness. Add flour as needed. If dough is hard to roll, let stand for 5 minutes and try again.

Preheat oven to 400 degrees. Coat two large pizza pans with non-stick cooking spray and lightly flour. Place rolled pizza dough on pans. Layer on pizza:

Pizza sauce
Toppings of your choice (precooked very lean ground meat, chopped green peppers, onions, mushrooms, etc.)
Part-skim mozzarella cheese

Bake for 12 to 20 minutes, depending on the thickness of your crust and desired crispness. Bottom should be lightly browned and cheese, bubbly.

Variations: You can make your own pizza sauce rather than buy-ing store-bought. See below. Skip the rising time if you're in a hurry, but expect a slightly tougher crust.

Tips: Carol Schlitt, the extension educator who nutritionally ana-lyzed this recipe, included 1 pound of ground beef in her analysis. To cut the fat content considerably (as we do), I use 2 to 4 ounces total for two pizzas.

Nutritional Data for One Serving (3 large slices): Calories: 777, Calories from Fat: 247, Total Fat: 27 g, Saturated Fat: 11 g, Cholesterol: 102 mg, Sodium: 1,115 mg, Total Carbohydrate: 85 g, Dietary Fiber: 7 g, Sugars: 11 g, Protein: 48 g, Vitamin A: 22% RDA, Vitamin C: 83% RDA, Calcium: 41% RDA, Iron: 40% RDA

Pizza Sauce

Combine and mix thoroughly:

> **2 8-ounce cans tomato sauce**
> **½ cup ketchup**
> **1 tablespoon Italian seasoning**
> **Honey or sugar to taste**

Poached Fish

Serves a versatile number

Adapted from a recipe by "seafood expert" and
longtime friend, Sally Davis.

Preheat oven to 400 degrees. Place in a large ovenproof pan:

> **"Meaty" fish (salmon, halibut, swordfish, or other fish that
> will hold together while cooking) portions**

Measure fish at the thickest part. Barely cover fish with:

> **Lightly salted water or water seasoned with herbs and
> spices or milk (choose only one option)**

Make sure oven is hot before fish goes in. Bake 10 minutes for every inch of thickness measured. Fish should flake easily.

Variations: Poached fish can be served hot, as an entree, with the sauce made by poaching. Or serve as the main ingredient of a casserole. Chilled and flaked, poached fish makes a delicious salad.

Tips: Eating fish is an important part of a healthy diet, but it can be expensive. Buy on sale, or ask the meat manager for suggestions of cheaper alternatives to a particular kind of fish you like.

Nutritional Data for One Serving (4 ounces): Calories: 165, Calories from Fat: 37, Total Fat: 4 g, Saturated Fat: 1 g, Cholesterol: 42 mg, Sodium: 102 mg, Total Carbohydrate: 4 g, Dietary Fiber: 0 g, Sugars: 4 g, Protein: 26 g, Vitamin A: 10% RDA, Vitamin C: 1% RDA, Calcium: 15% RDA, Iron: 6% RDA

Pot "Pie"

Serves 6

Preheat oven to 350 degrees. Brown in a frying pan:

2 cups diced chicken (raw, with a little water, or precooked)
1 small onion, diced

When onion and chicken are both tender, add:

2 cups green beans, drained
1 8-ounce can tomato sauce
1 tablespoon Worcestershire sauce or soy sauce
1 teaspoon chili powder
1 teaspoon garlic
½ teaspoon salt
¼ teaspoon pepper

Coat a large, ovenproof casserole dish with nonstick cooking spray. Pour mixture into casserole dish. Top with:

3 cups mashed potatoes

Bake for 30 minutes, until heated through.

Variations: If you prefer, add more chili powder. (We keep our dishes pretty bland, by some people's standards.)

Tips: When you're in a hurry, use instant mashed potatoes. We usually plan to serve this dish two days after we have mashed potatoes as a side dish: I just make twice the usual amount. (By the way, I think this entree was supposed to originally have a pie crust on the bottom of it, and that's why it's called Pot "Pie.")

Nutritional Data for One Serving (a large plateful and more): Calories: 204, Calories from Fat: 62, Total Fat: 7 g, Saturated Fat: 2 g, Cholesterol: 43 mg, Sodium: 829 mg, Total Carbohydrate: 21 g, Dietary Fiber: 2 g, Sugars: 1 g, Protein: 16 g, Vitamin A: 9% RDA, Vitamin C: 22% RDA, Calcium: 6% RDA, Iron: 12% RDA

Red Beans and Rice

Serves a large crowd

Prepare:

2 pounds dry kidney beans

Sort through beans and eliminate "duds." In a large metal pan, cover beans with 2 inches of water and soak overnight. The next day, drain liquid from beans. Set aside. Heat in a large frying pan:

2 tablespoons canola or olive oil

Over medium heat, stir in and cook until tender:

2 medium onions, diced
1 medium green pepper, diced
3 medium garlic cloves, minced

Add beans. Stir in:

1 small ham hock (or bits of ham)
1 16-ounce can diced tomatoes
1 tablespoon molasses or honey
2 bay leaves

½ teaspoon oregano
Salt, pepper, and red pepper to taste; plan to add quite a bit

Add:

Enough water to cover everything in the pan

Bring to a boil. Reduce heat and simmer until beans are tender. Serve over brown rice.

Variations: Eliminate the ham hock and add more seasonings for a vegetarian dish. Substitute canned kidney beans for dried ones. The original recipe calls for smoked sausage (stirred in during the last 20 minutes of cooking), plus ½ teaspoon dried marjoram and ½ teaspoon dried thyme.

Tips: This dish can be spiced up considerably with the addition of a few shakes of hot sauce.

Nutritional Data for One Serving (a big, big bowl): Calories: 545, Calories from Fat: 71, Total Fat: 8 g, Saturated Fat: 1 g, Cholesterol: 2 mg, Sodium: 301 mg, Total Carbohydrate: 99 g, Dietary Fiber: 4 g, Sugars: 4 g, Protein: 22 g, Vitamin A: 4% RDA, Vitamin C: 41% RDA, Calcium: 16% RDA, Iron: 38% RDA

Salmon Croquettes

Serves 4 to 6

Combine in a bowl:

1 15-ounce can salmon
1 8-ounce can water-packed tuna
2 egg whites
¼ cup nonfat milk
1 cup crushed saltine crackers

Preheat oven to broil setting. Debone salmon and discard most of the liquid. Drain and discard liquid from tuna. Mix ingredients and shape mixture into small patties. Crush additional cracker crumbs and roll the patties in extra crumbs. Broil for about 10 minutes on one side, until nicely browned. Turn, and broil an additional 6 to 8 minutes. Croquettes should be crispy.

Variations: You can stretch the salmon mixture by changing this recipe as follows: Add 2 slices of finely shredded whole-wheat bread, 2 more egg whites, and enough liquid (milk and/or salmon juice) to moisten. Broil as usual. We sometimes fry the croquettes in canola oil.

Tips: If your family includes picky eaters, debone the salmon before mixing up croquettes.

Nutritional Data for One Serving (2 to 3 croquettes): Calories: 290, Calories from Fat: 84, Total Fat: 9 g, Saturated Fat: 2 g, Cholesterol: 55 mg, Sodium: 855 mg, Total Carbohydrate: 19 g, Dietary Fiber: 0 g, Sugars: 1 g, Protein: 32 g, Vitamin A: 3% RDA, Vitamin C: 0% RDA, Calcium: 24% RDA, Iron: 15% RDA

Saucy "Faux" Steaks

From *Healthy Exchanges Food Newsletter**

16 ounces ground 90% lean turkey or beef
6 tablespoons dried bread crumbs (1½ ounces)
¼ cup finely chopped onion
½ cup Healthy Choice ketchup
1¾ cups canned stewed tomatoes with juice (14½ ounce can)

In a large bowl, combine meat, bread crumbs, onion, and ¼ cup ketchup. Mix well. Using a full ⅓ cup measure as a guide, form into 6 patties. Place patties in a large skillet sprayed with butter-flavored cooking spray. Brown on both sides. In a small bowl, combine stewed tomatoes and remaining ¼ cup ketchup. Pour mixture evenly over meat. Lower heat. Cover and simmer 15 minutes. For each serving, place a piece of "steak" on plate and evenly spoon sauce over top. Freezes well.

Serves 6
Each serving equals:
HE: 2 Protein, ⅔ Vegetable, ⅓ Bread, ½ Slider
175 Calories, 7 gm Fat, 15 gm Protein, 13 gm Carbohydrate, 475 mg Sodium
Diabetic: 2 Meat, 1 Vegetable, ½ Starch
HINT: Good served with rice, pasta, or potatoes.

*Note: The format of this recipe differs from most others in this book at JoAnna Lund's—the author's—request that her original recipe remain exactly as it appeared in her newsletter.

Spaghetti

Serves 6

Prepare according to package directions:

16 ounces spaghetti or similar pasta

Set aside. Combine in a large frying pan:

3 8-ounce cans tomato sauce
1 16-ounce can crushed tomatoes
2 tablespoons Italian seasoning
1 tablespoon molasses

Simmer for about 30 minutes, until mixture is thick and bubbly. Serve hot over spaghetti.

Variations: Add diced meat to spaghetti sauce.
Tips: Spaghetti can be brought to a boil, covered immediately, heat turned off, then left to stand for several hours. The pasta will finish cooking itself.

Nutritional Data for One Serving (2 medium plates, filled): Calories: 347, Calories from Fat: 15, Total Fat: 2 g, Saturated Fat: 0 g, Cholesterol: 0 mg, Sodium: 871 mg, Total Carbohydrate: 72 g, Dietary Fiber: 2 g, Sugars: 4 g, Protein: 12 g, Vitamin A: 21% RDA, Vitamin C: 36% RDA, Calcium: 10% RDA, Iron: 32% RDA

Steamed Fish in Foil

Serves 6

Preheat oven to 400 degrees. Cut six 12-inch squares of aluminum foil. Place in the center of each square:

1 4-ounce fillet of turbot or other white-fleshed fish (24 ounces total)
1 large mushroom (6 total), sliced
2 thin slices of onion (1 medium onion total)
½ tablespoon fresh chopped dill (3 tablespoons total)
1 tablespoon water (about ¾ cup total)
Salt and black pepper

Measure fish fillet at thickest part. Turn foil edges upward to create a cup. Seal top of foil completely shut. Place foil packets on baking sheet. Bake in preheated oven, allowing 10 minutes for each inch of thickness (round it out to the nearest inch, average).

Variations: Add thinly sliced potatoes and carrots, precooked in the microwave.

Tips: Open the foil packets carefully; the steam can burn you.

Nutritional Data for One Serving (1 packet): Calories: 122, Calories from Fat: 31, Total Fat: 3 g, Saturated Fat: 0 g, Cholesterol: 54 mg, Sodium: 527 mg, Total Carbohydrate: 3 g, Dietary Fiber: 1 g, Sugars: 1 g, Protein: 19 g, Vitamin A: 1% RDA, Vitamin C: 7% RDA, Calcium: 3% RDA, Iron: 4% RDA

Stir-Fry

Serves 6 to 8

Slice into thin strips:

**4 cups carrots, onions, zucchini, cucumbers, sweet
potatoes, broccoli, and/or other fresh produce**

Set aside. In a large nonstick frying pan, heat:

1 tablespoon olive or canola oil

When oil is hot enough to sizzle a drop of water, quickly sauté vegetables to desired doneness. Stir in:

2 tablespoons soy sauce
2 tablespoons chunky peanut butter
2 cloves garlic, finely minced

Simmer. Combine in an airtight plastic bowl:

2 tablespoons cornstarch
1 cup water

Shake the cornstarch and water together until smooth. Add to vegetables. Bring to a boil, stirring constantly, for 1 minute. Turn down heat and add a small amount of cooked leftover chicken. Serve hot over brown rice.

Variations: I like to use this recipe when I'm ready to clean up leftovers, as you can toss in nearly anything on hand. It's not as Asian with green beans and potatoes, of course, but still tastes good. Most kinds of meat or combinations of meats, used very sparingly, work well, or meat can be left out entirely.

Tips: To cut down on fat even more, eliminate the peanut butter.

Nutritional Data for One Serving (a big plateful): Calories: 266, Calories from Fat: 53, Total Fat: 6 g, Saturated Fat: 1 g, Cholesterol: 0 mg, Sodium: 349 mg, Total Carbohydrate: 48 g, Dietary Fiber: 5 g, Sugars: 4 g, Protein: 6 g, Vitamin A: 88% RDA, Vitamin C: 29% RDA, Calcium: 5% RDA, Iron: 8% RDA

Susan Thomas's Casserole

Serves 12 to 15

Adapted from a recipe in *Dinner's in the Freezer,* by Jill Bond.

Brown in a large frying pan:

**1½ pounds ground chuck or ground turkey
1 cup onion, chopped**

When meat is cooked and onions are tender, drain grease. Preheat oven to 350 degrees. Prepare according to package directions:

1 10-ounce package noodles

Set aside. Add to meat and onion mixture:

**1 16-ounce can corn
1 can cream of chicken soup
1 can cream of mushroom soup
1 cup nonfat yogurt
¼ cup chopped pimento
1½ teaspoons salt
½ teaspoon pepper
Cooked noodles**

Mix thoroughly. Pour into two medium-size, ovenproof casserole dishes. Bake for 30 minutes.

Variations and Tips: Jill Mega-cooks, so her basic recipe (above) yields two meals (12 to 15 servings). She goes further in each of her recipes, as in this one, when she increases the yield to six meals. The ingredients are:

**1 family pack of ground turkey or beef (approximately 10 to 12 pounds)
5 to 6 cups chopped onion
1 #10 can kernel corn, drained
2 large cans (26 ounces) cream of chicken soup
2 large cans (26 ounces) cream of mushroom soup**

1 large carton (3 pounds) of sour cream (I changed this to nonfat yogurt)
1 large package (40 ounces) cooked noodles

Instructions are the same until after the ingredients are mixed; at that point, everything's divided into six casserole dishes, labeled, carefully wrapped, and frozen (before cooking). Each dish is thawed before serving, then baked.

Nutritional Data for One Serving (a generous plateful): Calories: 276, Calories from Fat: 106, Total Fat: 12 g, Saturated Fat: 4 g, Cholesterol: 45 mg, Sodium: 856 mg, Total Carbohydrate: 29 g, Dietary Fiber: 1 g, Sugars: 2 g, Protein: 15 g, Vitamin A: 23% RDA, Vitamin C: 145% RDA, Calcium: 7% RDA, Iron: 78% RDA

Sweet 'n' Sour Meatballs

Serves 8 to 10

Adapted from a recipe in *Dinner's in the Freezer,* by Jill Bond.

Mix together in a large bowl:

2 pounds lean ground beef or ground turkey
2 egg whites
Salt, pepper, onion salt, and garlic powder, as desired

Form mixture into 1-inch balls (try to get 32 to 40 from 2 pounds of meat). Brown meatballs in a large nonstick skillet until "done." Drain grease. Set aside. In a small pan, sauté in a little water until tender:

1 green pepper, cut into 1-inch strips

Set aside. Open:

2 cans (16 ounces each) chunk pineapple

Drain pineapple, reserving liquid in a watertight plastic container. Add to this container:

2 tablespoons cornstarch or flour

Put lid on container and shake vigorously until lumps are gone. Pour liquid into another saucepan. Add:

4 tablespoons vinegar (white or cider)
2 tablespoons sugar (white or brown)
1 tablespoon soy sauce

Bring to a boil, stirring constantly, until sauce becomes thick. Combine meatballs, pineapple chunks, green pepper, and sauce in the original large skillet (the one you used to cook the meat). Heat through.

Variations: Jill uses granulated fructose instead of sugar. She also adds raw green peppers to the recipe rather than sautéeing them first.

Tips: If sauce seems too thick, thin with a little juice or water. My family loves this recipe.

Nutritional Data for One Serving (4 meatballs): Calories: 325, Calories from Fat: 156, Total Fat: 17 g, Saturated Fat: 7 g, Cholesterol: 67 mg, Sodium: 661 mg, Total Carbohydrate: 23 g, Dietary Fiber: 1 g, Sugars: 18 g, Protein: 20 g, Vitamin A: 2% RDA, Vitamin C: 54% RDA, Calcium: 3% RDA, Iron: 14% RDA

Tuna Salad

Serves 4 to 6

Combine in a bowl:

1 large can water-packed tuna
2 hard-boiled eggs, yolks discarded, diced
4 tablespoons nonfat or low-fat mayonnaise
1 tablespoon sweet relish
1 tablespoon sugar

Chill thoroughly. Serve on oven-toasted whole-wheat buns or French bread.

Variations: Add extra nonfat mayonnaise if a creamier texture is desired. Substitute diced chicken or turkey for tuna. Substitute all egg whites for meat, and add ½ teaspoon paprika.
Tips: Serve stuffed in peppers, celery, or tomatoes.

Nutritional Data for One Serving (enough to fill a sandwich): Calories: 111, Calories from Fat: 33, Total Fat: 4 g, Saturated Fat: 0 g, Cholesterol: 19 mg, Sodium: 231 mg, Total Carbohydrate: 4 g, Dietary Fiber: 0 g, Sugars: 2 g, Protein: 14 g, Vitamin A: 1% RDA, Vitamin C: 0% RDA, Calcium: 1% RDA, Iron: 5% RDA

Turkey-Broccoli Casserole

Serves 6 to 8

(Read the entire page before you begin to cook.)

Here's the traditional recipe. Notice how I change it in the second section.
Preheat oven to 350 degrees. Combine in a saucepan:

**1 can cream of chicken soup
1 cup chicken or turkey broth
1 8-ounce package Velveeta cheese**

Heat, stirring occasionally, until cheese melts. Set aside. In a separate saucepan, cook until almost tender:

1 package frozen broccoli

Set aside. Dice into small pieces:

1 to 2 cups leftover turkey

Set aside. In a bowl, prepare:

1 package stuffing mix

Place in a greased casserole dish as follows: diced turkey, broccoli, cheese sauce. Top with stuffing. Bake for 20 to 30 minutes, until cheese bubbles and stuffing is lightly browned on top.

Variations and Tips: This recipe can be easily altered to save money and increase nutrition, with little additional time required. Here's my version of the casserole:

Shake together in an airtight container:

1 cup skim milk
3 tablespoons flour
Dash of both salt and pepper

Heat in a saucepan, stirring until bubbly. Add:

½ cup low-fat mozzarella cheese, shredded
2 tablespoons soy sauce

Cook and stir just until smooth and thickened. Set aside. Steam until tender:

1 medium head fresh broccoli, diced

Dice:

1 cup cooked turkey

Place in a nonstick casserole dish as follows: diced turkey, broccoli, cheese sauce. Top with:

2 cups homemade croutons

Bake for 20 to 30 minutes, until cheese bubbles and stuffing is lightly browned on top. This version is cheaper and healthier, and it takes about 5 more minutes to assemble than the original recipe.

Nutritional Data for One Serving (based on my version, about 1 cup): Calories: 125, Calories from Fat: 23, Total Fat: 3 g, Saturated Fat: 1 g, Cholesterol: 19 mg, Sodium: 475 mg, Total Carbohydrate: 13 g, Dietary Fiber: 2 g, Sugars: 2 g, Protein: 12 g, Vitamin A: 10% RDA, Vitamin C: 28% RDA, Calcium: 8% RDA, Iron: 7% RDA

Turkey Burgers

Serves 8

Adapted from a recipe in *Cheap Eating,* by Pat Edwards.

Combine in a large bowl:

1 pound ground turkey
4 egg whites
½ cup dry oats
⅓ cup ketchup
1 medium onion, finely chopped
1 teaspoon garlic powder

Form into patties. "Fry" in a skillet coated generously with nonstick cooking spray, until nicely browned.

Variations: When trying this recipe, I broiled the burgers rather than frying them. I also omitted the rest of the original recipe, which you may want to include:

Flip and place on each burger:

1 slice Swiss cheese (8 total)

Mix together:

2 tablespoons horseradish
½ cup (nonfat) mayonnaise

Spread mayo mix on a rye bread or bun and top with a burger.

Tips: I once used this recipe to make meatloaf. I coated muffin pans with nonstick cooking spray, added enough meat to fill each cup, and baked them in a 400-degree oven for about 25 minutes. We liked the "meatloaf cups" even better than the burgers.

Nutritional Data for One Serving (1 burger): Calories: 136, Calories from Fat: 50, Total Fat: 6 g, Saturated Fat: 1 g, Cholesterol: 45 mg, Sodium: 68 mg, Total Carbohydrate: 8 g, Dietary Fiber: 2 g, Sugars: 1 g, Protein: 13 g, Vitamin A: 0% RDA, Vitamin C: 2% RDA, Calcium: 2% RDA, Iron: 7% RDA

Vegetable Beef Soup

Serves 6 to 8

Combine in a Crock-Pot slow cooker:

1 15-ounce can tomatoes
2 carrots, sliced
2 stalks celery, sliced
2 medium onions, diced
2 medium potatoes, peeled and diced
3 cups water
1 teaspoon salt
4 whole peppercorns
3 beef bouillon cubes

Cover and cook on low for 12 to 24 hours.

Variations: Use this soup as a catchall for whatever is in your freezer or refrigerator. The last time I made it, I added leftover ham broth, a little broccoli, a can of green beans, one frozen tomato, and some odds-and-ends vegetables to the ingredients above. Instead of a slow cooker, combine the ingredients in a large kettle, and simmer on the stove all afternoon.

Tips: Serve topped with homemade croutons (see Recipe Index).

Nutritional Data for One Serving (2 bowls): Calories: 105, Calories from Fat: 3, Total Fat: 0 g, Saturated Fat: 0 g, Cholesterol: 0 mg, Sodium: 429 mg, Total Carbohydrate: 22 g, Dietary Fiber: 3 g, Sugars: 4 g, Protein: 5 g, Vitamin A: 62% RDA, Vitamin C: 46% RDA, Calcium: 4% RDA, Iron: 6% RDA

BREADS AND BREAKFAST FOODS

Bagels

Makes 12 bagels

Adapted from a recipe in *Cheap Eating,* by Pat Edwards.

Mix, until dissolved, in a large bowl:

⅔ cup very warm water
5 teaspoons dry yeast (or 2 packages)

Add:

1 cup whole-wheat flour
1 cup white flour
¾ cup water
2 tablespoons honey
1 tablespoon salt

Mix ingredients on high speed of electric mixer for 2 minutes. Reduce speed and gradually add:

2 cups white flour

When the dough becomes stiff, turn onto a floured board and knead by hand (or use a dough hook) until smooth. Place in a bowl lightly coated with nonstick cooking spray. Cover and let rest for 15 minutes. Divide dough into 12 balls. Pierce the center of each ball to make the center hole. Pull to enlarge. Let rise, covered, for 30 minutes on a baking sheet lightly coated with nonstick cooking spray. Preheat oven to 375 degrees. In a large saucepan, bring to a boil:

4 quarts water
1 teaspoon sugar

Reduce heat to simmer and add 4 bagels. After 3 minutes, turn and simmer 4 minutes longer. Remove. Pat dry and place on lightly sprayed baking sheet. Repeat with the remaining bagels. Bake for 30 minutes.

Variations: Add either cinnamon or onion flakes to the bagel dough.

Tips: These take time, but are really delicious, much better than store-bought. The next time we make them, I intend to make a huge batch and freeze a few.

Nutritional Data for One Serving (1 bagel): Calories: 165, Calories from Fat: 5, Total Fat: 1g, Saturated Fat: 0 g, Cholesterol: 0 mg, Sodium: 535 mg, Total Carbohydrate: 35 g, Dietary Fiber: 2 g, Sugars: 3 g, Protein: 5 g, Vitamin A: 0% RDA, Vitamin C: 0% RDA, Calcium: 1% RDA, Iron: 11% RDA

Banana Bread

Makes 3 thin loaves, about 10 slices per loaf

Preheat oven to 350 degrees. Coat 3 loaf pans with nonstick cooking spray, then lightly flour.

Cream together in a large bowl:

1 cup sugar
8 very ripe bananas, diced
8 egg whites

In a separate bowl, sift together:

1¼ cups white flour
1 cup whole-wheat flour
2 teaspoons baking soda
1 teaspoon salt

Combine flour mixture with creamed mixture and blend thoroughly. Turn into pans. Bake for 40 to 50 minutes.

Variations: Add nuts and/or raisins.

Tips: Check for doneness by inserting a toothpick in three or four areas of the bread; if you go through a piece of banana, you may sink into a gooey spot and think the bread isn't done.

Nutritional Data for One Serving (1 Slice): Calories: 92, Calories from Fat: 3, Total Fat: 0 g, Saturated Fat: 0 g, Cholesterol: 0 mg, Sodium: 170 mg, Total Carbohydrate: 21 g, Dietary Fiber: 1 g, Sugars: 11 g, Protein: 2 g, Vitamin A: 0% RDA, Vitamin C: 5% RDA, Calcium: 1% RDA, Iron: 3% RDA

Banana-Cranberry Muffins

From *Healthy Exchanges Food Newsletter.* *

1½ cups flour
1 (4 serving) package Jell-O sugar-free instant
banana pudding mix
¼ cup Sprinkle Sweet or Sugar Twin
1 teaspoon baking powder
1 teaspoon baking soda
½ teaspoon JO's Apple Pie Spice**
1 cup chopped fresh cranberries
⅔ cup mashed bananas (2 ripe medium)
1 teaspoon vanilla extract
2 eggs or equivalent in egg substitute
½ cup unsweetened applesauce

Preheat oven to 350 degrees. In a large bowl, combine flour, dry pudding mix, Sprinkle Sweet, baking powder, baking soda, and JO's Apple Pie Spice. Add chopped cranberries. Mix well. In a small bowl, combine mashed bananas, vanilla extract, eggs, and applesauce. Add banana mixture to flour mixture. Mix just until combined. Spray muffin tins with butter-flavored cooking spray or line with muffin liners. Fill muffin wells. Bake 22 to 25 minutes or until muffins test done. Cool on wire rack. Freezes well.

Serves 8
Each serving equals:
HE: 1 Bread, ¾ Fruit, ¼ Protein (limited), 19 Optional Calories
154 Calories, 2 gm Fat, 4 gm Protein, 30 gm Carbohydrate, 325 mg Sodium, 2 gm Fiber
Diabetic: 1 Starch, 1 Fruit

HINT: (1) Substitute any reputable brand for JO's Apple Pie Spice. (2) Fill unused muffin wells with water. It protects the muffin tin and ensures even baking.

*Note: The format of this recipe differs from most others in this book at JoAnna Lund's—the author's—request that her original recipe remain exactly as it appeared in her newsletter.
**See Resources under "Miscellaneous Products" on how to order JO's Spices.

Breadsticks

About 24 sticks total

Preheat oven to 350 degrees. Spread:

Several slices of whole-wheat bread

on a cookie sheet. Coat with nonstick cooking spray. Sprinkle on:

Garlic powder, minced onion, paprika, or any other seasonings

Cut each slice into five or six narrow rectangles. Bake for about 10 minutes, or until bottom side is browned; turn over and bake another 5 to 10 minutes. Serve hot or cold.

Nutritional Data for One Serving (1 stick): Calories: 14, Calories from Fat: 2, Total Fat: 0 g, Saturated Fat: 0 g, Cholesterol: 0 mg, Sodium: 25 mg, Total Carbohydrate: 3 g, Dietary Fiber: 0 g, Sugars: 0 g, Protein: 1 g, Vitamin A: 1% RDA, Vitamin C: 0% RDA, Calcium: 0% RDA, Iron: 1% RDA

Breakfast Biscuits

From *Healthy Exchanges Food Newsletter.* *

1½ **cups Bisquick reduced-fat baking mix**
¼ **cup + 1 tablespoon Sprinkle Sweet or Sugar Twin**
½ **cup raisins**
¼ **cup Kraft fat-free mayonnaise**
¾ **cup water**
½ **teaspoon cinnamon**

Preheat oven to 415 degrees. In a medium bowl, combine baking mix, ¼ cup Sprinkle Sweet, and raisins. Add mayonnaise and water. Mix well to combine. Spray muffin tin with butter-flavored cooking spray. Fill 8 wells half full. In a small bowl, combine remaining 1 tablespoon Sprinkle Sweet and cinnamon. Evenly sprinkle mixture over biscuit. Cut mixture into biscuit with a knife. Bake 10 to 12 minutes. Cool on wire rack. Freezes well.

Serves 8
Each serving equals:
HE: 1 Bread, ½ Fruit, 9 Optional Calories
126 Calories, 2 gm Fat, 2 gm Protein, 25 gm Carbohydrate, 304 mg Sodium, 1 gm Fiber
Diabetic: 1 Starch, ½ Fruit

HINT: (1) Fill unused muffin wells with water. It protects the muffin tins and ensures even baking.

*Note: The format of this recipe differs from most others in this book at JoAnna Lund's—the author's—request that her original recipe remain exactly as it appeared in her newsletter.

Cinnamon Yeast Bread (90-Minute Bread)

Makes 4 loaves

Dissolve together in a small, shallow bowl:

1 cup very warm water
4 packages (or 3 tablespoons) yeast

Set aside. In a large bowl, combine:

3 cups very warm water
4 teaspoons salt
3 tablespoons honey
4 tablespoons olive or canola oil

Combine the two mixtures. Stir in thoroughly:

4 cups whole-wheat flour
5 cups white flour

Add extra flour a little at a time, just enough to form a soft dough. Knead by pounding dough vigorously with a large spoon for 1 minute. (This is not a mistake.) Form four mounds of dough and let stand. One at a time, roll out each mound with a rolling pin on a floured surface to form a rectangle. Sprinkle on each rectangle:

1 tablespoon brown sugar (4 tablespoons total)
½ teaspoon cinnamon (2 teaspoons total)

Start at one of the long ends of each rectangle and roll up tightly to form compact loaves. Tuck loose ends under, seam sides down. Place in four bread pans coated with nonstick cooking spray. Let rise, covered in a warm place, for 30 minutes. Bake in preheated 350 degree oven for 30 to 40 minutes.

Variations: This bread can be baked as plain whole wheat bread by eliminating the rolling-out procedure: simply smooth out the dough and place it directly into pans for rising. If you don't mind a longer rising time, you can use half the amount of yeast.

Tips: This is one of our favorite recipes, absolutely delicious. From start to finish, it takes only 90 minutes or less. It is sometimes difficult to tell when the bread is really done, and you may have to actually cut a loaf in half to make sure there are no doughy areas. Extra loaves freeze well.

Nutritional Data for One Serving (1 slice): Calories: 122, Calories from Fat: 17, Total Fat: 2 g, Saturated Fat: 0 g, Cholesterol: 0 mg, Sodium: 215 mg, Total Carbohydrate: 23 g, Dietary Fiber: 2 g, Sugars: 1 g, Protein: 4 g, Vitamin A: 0% RDA, Vitamin C: 0% RDA, Calcium: 1% RDA, Iron: 8% RDA

Corn Bread (Muffins)

Serves 12

Adapted from a recipe in *A Taste of Dutch,* a cookbook by Jan Kent.

Preheat oven to 400 degrees. Mix together:

2 cups cornmeal
1 cup whole-wheat flour
1 cup white flour
¾ cup dry milk powder
4 tablespoons brown sugar
6 teaspoons baking powder
1 teaspoon salt

Set aside. In another bowl, mix together:

6 beaten egg whites
2 cups skim milk
¼ cup applesauce
¼ cup canola or olive oil

Add wet ingredients to dry ingredients, stirring just until smooth. Do not beat. Pour into a 9-x-13-inch pan coated with nonstick cooking spray. Bake for 25 to 30 minutes.

Variations: To make muffins, pour corn bread into muffin tins coated with nonstick cooking spray. Bake for about 15 to 20 minutes, until tops are golden brown.

Tips: Be careful not to overmix, or your cornbread will be dry and crumbly; this recipe is surprisingly moist. Serve with honey or all-fruit spread.

Nutritional Data for One Serving (1 large square): Calories: 254, Calories from Fat: 48, Total Fat: 5 g, Saturated Fat: 0 g, Cholesterol: 2 mg, Sodium: 253 mg, Total Carbohydrate: 42 g, Dietary Fiber: 3 g, Sugars: 2 g, Protein: 9 g, Vitamin A: 6% RDA, Vitamin C: 2% RDA, Calcium: 11% RDA, Iron: 10% RDA

Croutons

Fills a quart jar, about 16 servings

Preheat oven to 350 degrees. Dice into small cubes:

8 slices thick bread

Place in a large bowl. Sprinkle on:

Garlic powder, minced onions, paprika, and/or other seasonings, as desired

Coat bread cubes lightly with nonstick cooking spray. Toss gently. Turn onto nonstick cookie sheet. Bake for 20 to 30 minutes, stirring occasionally, until crisp.

Variations: Experiment with several seasonings until you find a taste your family loves.

Tips: Slightly dry bread works a little better than fresh. I keep a plastic bag in the freezer for storing bread ends and leftovers; when the bag is full, I have just enough for a batch of breadsticks or croutons.

Nutritional Data for One Serving (about ½ slice of bread): Calories: 41, Calories from Fat: 7, Total Fat: 1 g, Saturated Fat: 0 g, Cholesterol: 0 mg, Sodium: 75 mg, Total Carbohydrate: 8 g, Dietary Fiber: 0 g, Sugars: 0 g, Protein: 2 g, Vitamin A: 3% RDA, Vitamin C: 1% RDA, Calcium: 1% RDA, Iron: 3% RDA

Dill/Cottage Cheese Bread

Makes 2 loaves

Combine in a small bowl:

½ cup very warm water
2 packages (or 5 teaspoons) dry yeast

Set aside. In a separate bowl, combine:

4 tablespoons sugar (or 3 tablespoons honey)
2 tablespoons melted margarine
1 tablespoon dry minced onion
2 teaspoons dill weed
2 teaspoons salt
½ teaspoon baking soda
4 egg whites

Combine two mixtures. Heat in a saucepan until lukewarm:

2 cups low-fat cottage cheese

Add cottage cheese to other ingredients. Slowly add, a little at a time:

3 cups white flour
2 cups whole-wheat flour

Blend well. Cover. Let rise for 50 to 60 minutes in a warm place until doubled in size. Coat two loaf pans with nonstick cooking spray. Divide dough into two pans. Let rise for 30 to 40 minutes. Bake in a preheated 350 degree oven for 30 minutes, until golden brown.

Variations: The original recipe calls for 4 teaspoons dill seed in place of 2 teaspoons dill weed; I like this milder version better.
Tips: This is a moist, hearty bread, really tasty.

Nutritional Data for One Serving (1 slice): Calories:157, Calories from Fat: 18, Total Fat: 2 g, Saturated Fat: 1 g, Cholesterol: 2 mg, Sodium: 349 mg, Total Carbohydrate: 27 g, Dietary Fiber: 2 g, Sugars: 3 g, Protein: 8 g, Vitamin A: 2% RDA, Vitamin C: 0% RDA, Calcium: 3% RDA, Iron: 8% RDA

French Bread

Makes 4 loaves

In a small bowl, dissolve:

2 packages (or 5 teaspoons) dry yeast
1 cup very warm water

In a larger bowl, combine:

2 cups very warm water
2 tablespoons sugar (or 1½ tablespoons honey)
2 tablespoons olive or canola oil
3 teaspoons salt

Add second mixture to the first and mix well. Gradually stir in:

5 cups white flour
3 cups whole-wheat flour

Work through dough with a large spoon until blended. Add extra flour if needed. Let set for 10 minutes. Stir again thoroughly with spoon. Repeat the stirring process every 10 minutes for three more times, a total of five times in 1 hour. Turn dough onto floured surface and divide into four pieces. Shape into balls and let rise for 10 minutes. Roll out flat, then roll up firmly. Place on cookie sheets. Score diagonally five times on each top. Let rise until doubled. Bake in a preheated 400 degree oven for 30 to 35 minutes.

Variations: Use 4 cups each of whole-wheat and white flour for a lighter bread.

Tips: Lightly coat the bread tops with butter-flavor cooking spray during the last 10 minutes of baking for a golden crust. Freeze extra loaves.

Nutritional Data for One Serving (1 slice): Calories: 98, Calories from Fat: 9, Total Fat: 1 g, Saturated Fat: 0 g, Cholesterol: 0 mg, Sodium: 161 mg, Total Carbohydrate: 19 g, Dietary Fiber: 2 g, Sugars: 1 g, Protein: 3 g, Vitamin A: 0% RDA, Vitamin C: 0% RDA, Calcium: 1% RDA, Iron: 6% RDA

French Toast

Serves 6

Adapted from a recipe in *The $30 a Week Grocery Budget, Volume I,* by Donna McKenna.

Combine in a pie pan:

1⅓ cups skim milk
4 egg whites

Beat together with a whisk until foamy. Set aside. Preheat a large, nonstick frying pan until moderately hot, then coat with nonstick cooking spray. Dip each side of:

12 pieces of bread

in the egg wash very quickly (don't let it soak) and immediately place in the hot pan. Turn once, when underside is golden brown. Remove from pan when the other side browns. Add more nonstick cooking spray and dipped bread slices until all the egg/milk liquid is used.

Variations: Top with cinnamon and/or sugar, molasses, or honey. Or try this fancy brunch recipe: Spread fat-free cream cheese or strawberry preserves between 2 slices of bread. Dip top and bottom in egg wash (above) and sprinkle lightly with cinnamon. "Fry" in non-stick pan as usual. Cover a few minutes so heat penetrates middle filling.

Tips: Keep your pan well coated with cooking spray, as the bread slices stick easily.

Nutritional Data for One Serving (2 slices): Calories: 165, Calories from Fat: 18, Total Fat: 2 g, Saturated Fat: 0 g, Cholesterol: 1 mg, Sodium: 335 mg, Total Carbohydrate: 28 g, Dietary Fiber: 0 g, Sugars: 2 g, Protein: 8 g, Vitamin A: 3% RDA, Vitamin C: 1% RDA, Calcium: 12% RDA, Iron: 9% RDA

Granola

Serves 4

In a large, heavy skillet (preferably cast iron), pour:

3 cups uncooked rolled oats

Turn on heat to medium low and stir constantly for 15 minutes. Sprinkle in:

¼ cup (packed) brown sugar
¼ teaspoon salt

Cook for a few more minutes, still stirring. Remove from heat. Serve hot or cold.

Variations: Add wheat germ, sesame seeds, nuts, coconut, raisins, etc. to your granola. (I kept mine simple, low-fat, and cheap.)

Tips: This granola is so good it's worth the long stirring time. (You can read a book while you stand at the stove.) I like it better than the heavy-syrup version.

Nutritional Data for One Serving (¾ cup): Calories: 285, Calories from Fat: 34, Total Fat: 4 g, Saturated Fat: 1 g, Cholesterol: 0 mg, Sodium: 141 mg, Total Carbohydrate: 54 g, Dietary Fiber: 6 g, Sugars: 1 g, Protein: 10 g, Vitamin A: 1% RDA, Vitamin C: 0% RDA, Calcium: 4% RDA, Iron: 16% RDA

Healthy Bran Muffins

Serves 8

Adapted from a recipe by Jan Kent, author of
the *A Taste of Dutch* cookbook.

Preheat oven to 400 degrees. Mix together in a large bowl:

2 cups whole-wheat flour
1 cup bran, flakes or raw
2 tablespoons baking powder
1 teaspoon salt

Set aside. Beat together in a separate bowl:

4 egg whites
2 cups skim milk
½ cup molasses
½ cup applesauce

Add dry ingredients to eggs/milk mixture, and stir just well enough to moisten flour. Coat muffin tins with nonstick cooking spray. Fill ⅔ full. Bake for about 15 minutes, until nicely browned.

Variations: Add raisins or diced dates to the batter. Once, when I made this recipe, I was out of bran and substituted 1 cup of bran cereal (it worked). Add more molasses for sweeter muffins.

Tips: I usually double or triple this recipe and freeze the extras for breakfasts.

Nutritional Data for One Serving (2 muffins): Calories: 205, Calories from Fat: 8, Total Fat: 1 g, Saturated Fat: 0 g, Cholesterol: 1 mg, Sodium: 396 mg, Total Carbohydrate: 43 g, Dietary Fiber: 5 g, Sugars: 4 g, Protein: 9 g, Vitamin A: 4% RDA, Vitamin C: 3% RDA, Calcium: 26% RDA, Iron: 29% RDA

Nut Raisin Bread

Makes 2 loaves

Preheat oven to 325 degrees. Combine in a medium-size saucepan:

2 cups raisins
1 cup water

Bring to a boil; turn off heat, and cool. Combine in a large bowl:

4 cups whole-wheat flour
1 tablespoon baking soda
1 teaspoon salt

Set aside. In another large bowl, combine:

2 cups honey
8 egg whites
¼ cup olive or canola oil
2 teaspoons vanilla

Beat until well-blended. Set aside. Drain water from raisins. Add raisins, plus:

2 cups mashed bananas
1 cup pecans or walnuts, chopped

to honey mixture. Add flour mixture, stirring just to blend all ingredients. Do not overmix. Spray two loaf pans with nonstick cooking spray; divide batter between the two pans. Bake for 1 hour. Lower oven temperature to 250 degrees and continue to bake for an additional 30 minutes, or until a wooden toothpick inserted in center comes out clean.

Variations: Omit nuts and/or reduce raisins, for cheaper, lower-fat bread.

Tips: The final bread is dark and dense, with a very "healthy" taste.

Nutritional Data for One Serving (1 slice): Calories: 310, Calories from Fat: 64, Total Fat: 7 g, Saturated Fat: 1 g, Cholesterol: 0 mg, Sodium: 290 mg, Total Carbohydrate: 63 g, Dietary Fiber: 4 g, Sugars: 14 g, Protein: 5 g, Vitamin A: 0% RDA, Vitamin C: 5% RDA, Calcium: 2% RDA, Iron: 9% RDA

Oatmeal Pancakes

Serves 4 to 6

Combine in a large bowl:

 2 cups whole-wheat flour
 ½ cup brown sugar
 4 teaspoons baking powder
 ½ teaspoon salt

Set aside. In another bowl, beat together:

 4 egg whites
 1 cup raw oats (or leftover cooked oatmeal)
 2 cups skim milk
 ¼ cup canola or olive oil
 ¼ cup applesauce

Combine the two mixtures and blend until smooth. For each pancake, pour ¼ cup batter onto a hot, nonstick skillet. Cook until bubbles begin to form on top, turn, and brown other side.

Variations: This recipe is very flexible. Make the batter thicker or thinner, as you prefer. For a treat, add chocolate chips, nuts, or bits of banana. Omit cooked oatmeal, or replace it with ¾ cup dry oats soaked in ½ cup hot water.

Tips: These pancakes are so moist you don't need syrup. I usually serve them with a dusting of powdered sugar on top. But if you prefer, make the easy, rich, low-fat syrup recipe that follows.

Nutritional Data for One Serving (5 or 6 3-inch pancakes): Calories: 429, Calories from Fat: 112, Total Fat: 12 g, Saturated Fat: 1 g, Cholesterol: 2 mg, Sodium: 332 mg, Total Carbohydrate: 69 g, Dietary Fiber: 7 g, Sugars: 5 g, Protein: 14 g, Vitamin A: 6% RDA, Vitamin C: 4% RDA, Calcium: 19% RDA, Iron: 15% RDA

Pancake Syrup

Combine in a saucepan:

3 cups brown sugar
1½ cups water

Bring to a boil and stir occasionally, until sugar dissolves. Remove from heat. Stir in:

1 teaspoon vanilla

Serve hot or cold.

Popovers

Makes 12 popovers

Adapted from a recipe in *The $30 a Week Grocery Budget,*
Volume I, by Donna McKenna.

Preheat oven to 450 degrees. Combine in a large bowl:

1 cup whole-wheat flour
1 cup white flour
3 tablespoons sugar (or 2 tablespoons honey)
4 egg whites
2 cups skim milk

Coat a 12-count muffin tin with nonstick cooking spray. Fill ⅓ full with popover batter. Bake at 450 degrees for 10 minutes, then reduce heat to 350 degrees and bake for an additional 15 to 20 minutes.

Variations: Popovers can be served as is, with all-fruit jam, or stuffed with nearly anything imaginable: diced meats, vegetables, cheeses, fruit mixtures, puddings, etc. We enjoy them plain, but these moist, delicious rolls could be the base for a main dish.

Tips: I like this recipe because it's fast, easy, and good. Do not open the oven until after 30 minutes of baking or the popovers may fall. It's a little tricky to get them to "puff." It may take you a few tries before you're able to make this work, but even flattened popovers taste wonderful. Do not use paper baking cups, and spray the pans generously with cooking spray, as the popovers really stick.

Nutritional Data for One Serving (2 popovers): Calories: 141, Calories from Fat: 6, Total Fat: 1 g, Saturated Fat: 0 g, Cholesterol: 1 mg, Sodium: 80 mg, Total Carbohydrate: 27 g, Dietary Fiber: 3 g, Sugars: 12 g, Protein: 8 g, Vitamin A: 5% RDA, Vitamin C: 1% RDA, Calcium: 11% RDA, Iron: 5% RDA

Poppy Seed Muffins

Makes about 2 dozen muffins

Preheat oven to 400 degrees. Mix together in a bowl:

1 cup whole-wheat flour
1 cup white flour
3 teaspoons poppy seeds
½ teaspoon salt
¼ teaspoon baking soda

In a separate bowl, combine:

1½ cups nonfat yogurt
1 cup sugar
4 egg whites
1 teaspoon vanilla

Cream together thoroughly. Combine the two mixtures. Coat two 12-count muffin tins with nonstick cooking spray. Spoon batter into muffin tins, filling each cup about ⅔ full. Bake for 15 to 20 minutes.

Variations: Poppy seeds can be omitted. Use plain yogurt or any flavor you prefer.

Tips: Buy your poppy seeds in bulk from a co-op or health food store for a tremendous savings. Homemade yogurt will also save you money (see Recipe Index).

Nutritional Data for One Serving (1 muffin): Calories: 110, Calories from Fat: 3, Total Fat: 0 g,

Saturated Fat: 0 g, Cholesterol: 0 mg, Sodium: 78 mg, Total Carbohydrate: 20 g, Dietary Fiber: 1 g, Sugars: 9 g, Protein: 3 g, Vitamin A: 0% RDA, Vitamin C: 0% RDA, Calcium: 4% RDA, Iron: 3% RDA

Pretzels

Makes 12 large pretzels

Adapted from a recipe in *Cheap Eating*, by Pat Edwards.

Preheat oven to 350 degrees. Combine in a small bowl:

1 package (or 2½ teaspoons) yeast
1⅓ cups warm water

Stir until yeast is dissolved. Add:

3 cups white flour
1 cup whole-wheat flour
1 teaspoon salt
½ teaspoon sugar

Knead, adding flour as necessary, to form an easy-to-handle dough. Coat large bowl with nonstick cooking spray. Place dough in bowl; let rise until doubled. Divide dough into 12 pieces. Roll pieces into 12-inch strings. Tie into knots. Brush with:

1 egg, beaten

Sprinkle on:

Coarse salt and/or onion flakes

Bake for 15 to 20 minutes, until golden brown.

Variations: Use all white flour instead of part white, part whole wheat.
Tips: Pat Edwards says making her pretzels is "a wonderful rainy-day activity to share with young children." I agree.

Nutritional Data for One Serving (1 pretzel): Calories: 158, Calories from Fat: 9, Total Fat: 1 g, Saturated Fat: 0 g, Cholesterol: 18 mg, Sodium: 1,251 mg, Total Carbohydrate: 32 g, Dietary Fiber: 2 g, Sugars: 0 g, Protein: 5 g, Vitamin A: 1% RDA, Vitamin C: 0% RDA, Calcium: 2% RDA, Iron: 10% RDA

Pumpkin/Zucchini Bread

Makes 2 loaves

Preheat oven to 325 degrees. Coat two loaf pans with nonstick cooking spray, then flour. Cream together in a large bowl:

1½ cups sugar
¾ cup applesauce
¼ cup canola or olive oil

Gradually add:

6 egg whites
2 teaspoons vanilla

Beat well. Grate:

3 cups pumpkin or zucchini

Add to sugar-and-oil mixture and blend well. In a separate bowl, combine:

1½ cups white flour
1½ cups whole-wheat flour
1 teaspoon cinnamon
1 teaspoon salt
1 teaspoon baking powder
1 teaspoon baking soda

Combine the two mixtures and blend well. Bake for 1 hour, or until toothpick inserted in the center comes out clean.

Variations: This recipe is an excellent way to use up garden vegetables; I have substituted squash, for example, with good results. Add nuts if you prefer. Substitute 1 cup extra pumpkin or zucchini in place of the applesauce and oil.

Tips: My children love this bread and often ask for seconds and thirds. It makes a good, nutritious snack and doesn't take long to make. I usually double the recipe and freeze 2 of the 4 loaves.

Nutritional Data for One Serving (1 slice): Calories: 170, Calories from Fat: 29, Total Fat: 3 g, Saturated Fat: 0 g, Cholesterol: 0 mg, Sodium: 190 mg, Total Carbohydrate: 33 g, Dietary Fiber: 3 g, Sugars: 15 g, Protein. 4 g, Vitamin A: 81% RDA, Vitamin C: 4% RDA, Calcium: 2% RDA, Iron: 7% RDA

Wheat Thins

Makes about four dozen small crackers

Adapted from a recipe in an out-of-print copy of
The Penny Pincher newsletter.

Preheat oven to 350 degrees. Mix together in a large bowl:

1¾ cups whole-wheat flour
1½ cups white flour

Set aside. Combine in a blender:

⅓ cup canola or olive oil
1 cup water
¾ teaspoon salt

Blend until oil and water mix. Add liquid to dry mixture. Knead just enough to combine ingredients, as little as possible, until dough is smooth. Roll out very thinly (no more than ⅛-inch thick) on an un-greased cookie sheet. Use a knife or a comb to mark the size of the crackers, being careful not to cut completely through dough. Prick each cracker three times with a fork. Bake for about 30 to 35 minutes, until crackers are light brown and crisp.

Variations: Use a variety of seasonings: poppy seeds, sesame seeds, onion powder, or salt, etc. to flavor the dough.

Tips: At first my children didn't care for the taste of these crackers, but they really grow on you. For picky eaters, replace some of the whole-wheat flour with white flour.

Nutritional Data for One Serving (1 large cracker): Calories: 42, Calories from Fat: 15, Total Fat: 2 g, Saturated Fat: 0 g, Cholesterol: 0 mg, Sodium: 34 mg, Total Carbohydrate: 6 g, Dietary Fiber: 1 g, Sugars: 0 g, Protein: 1 g, Vitamin A: 0% RDA, Vitamin C: 0% RDA, Calcium: 0% RDA, Iron: 2% RDA

SIDE DISHES

Alfalfa Sprouts

Makes one quart jar full of sprouts

Pour into a wide-mouthed quart jar:

About ¼ cup alfalfa seeds
Enough tepid water to cover the seeds (plus a little more)

Let sit for about 12 hours, or overnight. Cover lid of jar with cheese-cloth and secure with a heavy rubber band. Drain water into a bowl; reserve for watering houseplants (it has lots of vitamins and minerals). Fill jar again with tepid water. Immediately turn jar upside down, at a 45 degree angle, in a sturdy bowl or pan, so that water can drain out. Cover jar loosely with a dark plastic bag. Place in a dark area like a cupboard or bread box. Twice a day, fill the jar with water, then drain out. In a few days, the sprouts will be fully grown and ready to eat.

Variations and Tips: Sprouts are incredibly easy to grow, and very healthy. Spread out your rinsing times as much as possible. Serve in salads, on sandwiches, or in stir-fries and stews for extra nutrition and virtually no extra calories. Buy your seeds from a health food store or a cooperative.

Nutritional Data for One Serving (1 cup): Calories: 10, Calories from Fat: 2, Total Fat: 0 g, Saturated Fat: 0 g, Cholesterol: 0 mg, Sodium: 2 mg, Total Carbohydrate: 1 g, Dietary Fiber: 1 g, Sugars: 0 g, Protein: 1 g, Vitamin A: 1% RDA, Vitamin C: 5% RDA, Calcium: 1% RDA, Iron: 2% RDA

Basic Beans

Makes about 5 cups

Place in a large saucepan:

1 pound dried beans
1 teaspoon salt
About 8 cups water, enough to cover the beans

Soak overnight. In the morning, drain beans. Combine in the same large saucepan:

Soaked beans
1 teaspoon salt
8 more cups of water

Bring to a boil and boil for 10 minutes. Reduce heat. Cover and simmer 90 minutes or until beans are tender. Stir occasionally, adding more water if needed.

Variations and Tips: Cook presoaked beans in your Crock-Pot®, for 2 hours on high and 8 to 10 hours on low. Start with the above recipe, then use it as a base for others like those below.

Nutritional Data for One Serving (½ cup): Calories from Fat: 5, Total Fat: 1 g, Saturated Fat: 0 g, Cholesterol: 0 mg, Sodium: 413 mg, Total Carbohydrate: 58 g, Dietary Fiber: 7 g, Sugars: 4 g, Protein: 8 g, Vitamin A: 4% RDA, Vitamin C: 14% RDA, Calcium: 6% RDA, Iron: 17% RDA

Broiled Eggplant

Serves 4 to 6

Set oven temperature to broil. Mix together in a small, shallow bowl:

1 egg white
½ cup skim milk
½ cup flour
½ teaspoon salt
Dash of pepper

Stir until lump-free. Set aside. Coat broiler pan generously with non-stick cooking spray. Peel and slice thinly:

1 small eggplant (or part of eggplant)

Dip in batter; let excess drip off into batter bowl. Place dipped eggplant on broiler rack. Broil on one side until golden brown, about 5 minutes. Turn; broil until second side is browned, another 5 minutes.

Variations: Try this recipe with squash, tomatoes, or other similar garden vegetables.

Tips: I'm not much of an eggplant fan, but even I—and some of our children—like it served this way.

Nutritional Data for One Serving (about ½ cup): Calories: 32, Calories from Fat: 2, Total Fat: 0 g, Saturated Fat: 0 g, Cholesterol: 0 mg, Sodium: 198 mg, Total Carbohydrate: 6 g, Dietary Fiber: 0 g, Sugars: 1 g, Protein: 2 g, Vitamin A: 2% RDA, Vitamin C: 1% RDA, Calcium: 3% RDA, Iron: 1% RDA

Coleslaw

Serves 6 to 8

Shred into narrow strips:

½ medium cabbage
1 small onion

Mix well. Set aside. In a separate bowl, combine:

1 cup reduced-calorie Miracle Whip salad dressing or mayonnaise
½ cup nonfat yogurt
3 tablespoons sugar
1 teaspoon paprika

Pour creamy mixture over cabbage and onion. Mix thoroughly. Chill before serving.

Variations: If you prefer a more tart taste, add a little vinegar to the coleslaw.

Tips: Cabbage is usually cheap and always healthy, a good vegetable to serve often.

Nutritional Data for One Serving (about ½ cup): Calories: 154, Calories from Fat: 84, Total Fat: 9 g, Saturated Fat: 0 g, Cholesterol: 12 mg, Sodium: 245 mg, Total Carbohydrate: 16 g, Dietary Fiber: 2 g, Sugars: 9 g, Protein: 2 g, Vitamin A: 3% RDA, Vitamin C: 69% RDA, Calcium: 7% RDA, Iron: 2% RDA

French Fries

Serves 8

Scrub with a brush, peel (if desired), cut in half, then bake in a Crock-Pot slow cooker for 6 to 8 hours:

8 large Idaho potatoes

Preheat oven to 425 degrees. Slice potatoes into strips. Lightly coat large cookie sheet with nonstick cooking spray. Coat strips with cooking spray. Bake until "fries" are browned on one side, about 15 minutes; turn. Brown on second side, about 15 minutes.

Variations: For a more authentic taste, place cooked fries in a paper bag with a teaspoon or more of salt and shake thoroughly.

Nutritional Data for One Serving (about 1 cup): Calories: 183, Calories from Fat: 4, Total Fat: 0 g, Saturated Fat: 0 g, Cholesterol: 0 mg, Sodium: 17 mg, Total Carbohydrate: 41 g, Dietary Fiber: 4 g, Sugars: 0 g, Protein: 5 g, Vitamin A: 0% RDA, Vitamin C: 69% RDA, Calcium: 3% RDA, Iron: 19% RDA

Fresh Green Beans and Onions

Serves 4 to 6

Buy a "mess" of fresh green beans at the produce stand. Wash, snap off end pieces, and cut into bite-size pieces. Place in the Crock-Pot:

Prepared green beans
1 onion, thinly sliced and diced
Enough water to just cover the beans

Cook on high for several hours, until beans are tender.

Variations and Tips: The Crock-Pot slow cooker uses less energy than a stove, and it doesn't heat up your kitchen. But if you prefer, you can prepare these beans on a burner. Try the same simple recipe with other fresh vegetables. Save the liquid (if you don't serve it with the beans) in a "soup pot" in your freezer for future use.

Nutritional Data for One Serving (1 cup): Calories: 54, Calories from Fat: 4, Total Fat: 0 g, Saturated Fat: 0 g, Cholesterol: 0 mg, Sodium: 5 mg, Total Carbohydrate: 12 g, Dietary Fiber: 3 g, Sugars: 3 g, Protein: 3 g, Vitamin A: 8% RDA, Vitamin C: 23% RDA, Calcium: 6% RDA, Iron: 9% RDA

Frozen Fruit Delight

Serves 8 to 10

Combine in a blender:

2 large, very ripe bananas, cut into pieces
1 6-ounce can orange juice concentrate
1 small can crushed, water-packed pineapple
3 cups water

Blend until smooth. Pour thin layers into metal trays and freeze. Just before serving, slice into small pieces and thaw slightly.

Variations: The original recipe calls for 4 oranges with pulp (instead of orange juice), lemon juice, and 1½ cups of sugar. My variation is cheaper and more nutritious.

Tips: We often make Frozen Fruit Delight into ice pops.

Nutritional Data for One Serving (about ⅔ cup): Calories: 63, Calories from Fat: 2, Total Fat: 0 g, Saturated Fat: 0 g, Cholesterol: 0 mg, Sodium: 4 mg, Total Carbohydrate: 16 g, Dietary Fiber: 1 g, Sugars: 10 g, Protein: 1 g, Vitamin A: 1% RDA, Vitamin C: 44% RDA, Calcium: 1% RDA, Iron: 2% RDA

Fruit Salad

Serves as many as you like

Combine in a large glass bowl:

Canned peach slices (packed in their own juice)
White grapes
Fresh strawberries, diced
Bananas, sliced
Blueberries, when in season

Variations: Limitless.
Tips: Use whatever fruit is in season and save money.

Nutritional Data for One Serving: Too hard to figure, but with very few calories and no fat, this salad is healthy.

Golden Broccoli Salad

From *Healthy Exchanges Food Newsletter.**

3¼ cups chopped broccoli
1 cup shredded carrots
¼ cup chopped onion
¾ cup shredded Kraft reduced-fat cheddar cheese (3 ounces)
2 tablespoons Hormel Bacon Bits
¾ cup Kraft fat-free mayonnaise
Sugar substitute to equal 2 tablespoons sugar
1½ teaspoons prepared mustard
2 tablespoons skim milk

In a large bowl, combine broccoli, carrots, onion, cheddar cheese, and Bacon Bits. In a small bowl, combine mayonnaise, sugar substitute, mustard, and skim milk. Add mixture to broccoli mixture. Toss gently to combine. Cover and refrigerate until ready to serve.

Serves 6 (¾ cup)
Each serving equals:
HE: 1½ Vegetable, ⅔ Protein, ¼ Slider, 12 Optional Calories
99 Calories, 3 gm Fat, 7 gm Protein, 11 gm Carbohydrate, 404 mg Sodium, 2 gm Fiber
Diabetic: 2 Vegetable, ½ Meat

*Note: The format of this recipe differs from most others in this book at JoAnna Lund's—the author's—request that her original recipe remain exactly as it appeared in her newsletter.

Greek Feta Salad

From *Healthy Exchanges Food Newsletter.**

3 cups shredded lettuce
1¼ cups chopped cucumber
1 cup chopped tomato
½ cup chopped green bell pepper
¼ cup chopped onion
¾ cup cubed Feta cheese (3 ounces)
¼ cup sliced ripe olives (1 ounce)
2 tablespoons chopped fresh parsley
or 2 teaspoons dried parsley flakes
¼ cup Kraft fat-free Ranch dressing
2 tablespoons Kraft fat-free Italian dressing

In a large bowl, combine lettuce, cucumber, tomato, green pepper, onion, Feta cheese, olives, and parsley. Mix well. Cover and refrigerate. Just before serving, combine Ranch dressing and Italian dressing. Pour mixture over lettuce mixture. Toss gently to combine.

Serves 4 (2 cups)
Each serving equals:
HE: 3 Vegetable, 1 Protein, ¼ Fat, ¼ Slider, 7 Optional Calories
114 Calories, 5 gm Fat, 4 gm Protein, 13 gm Carbohydrate, 516 mg Sodium, 2 gm Fiber
Diabetic: 2 Vegetable, 1 Meat

HINT: If you can't find Feta cheese, use either reduced-fat Swiss cheese or any other cheese of your choice.

*Note: The format of this recipe differs from most others in this book at JoAnna Lund's—the author's—request that her original recipe remain exactly as it appeared in her newsletter.

Hashbrowns

Serves 6 to 8

Scrub, peel, halve, and cook in the Crock-Pot for 6 to 8 hours:

6 large potatoes

Cool for at least half an hour. Grate potatoes into a large bowl, and add:

1 large onion, grated

Heat a large, nonstick frying pan on the stove to medium hot. Mix potatoes and onions thoroughly and place grated potatoes and onions in hot pan. Cover. Cook for about 15 minutes, until underside is crispy and brown. Turn. Cook another 10 minutes. Add salt and pepper as desired.

Variations: Grate zucchini, squash, carrots, and/or bits of leftover vegetables into hashbrowns. Add diced chicken, and this side dish becomes an entree.

Tips: For a buttery taste, lightly coat potatoes (as they cook) with butter-flavored cooking spray.

Nutritional Data for One Serving (about ⅔ cup): Calories: 148, Calories from Fat: 3, Total Fat: 0 g, Saturated Fat: 0 g, Cholesterol: 0 mg, Sodium: 10 mg, Total Carbohydrate: 34 g, Dietary Fiber: 3 g, Sugars: 1 g, Protein: 3 g, Vitamin A: 4% RDA, Vitamin C: 37% RDA, Calcium: 1% RDA, Iron: 3% RDA

Lemon Gelatin Delight

Serves 8 to 10

Combine in a bowl:

> **2 small packages lemon gelatin**
> **4 cups boiling water**

Stir until dissolved. Pour into a 9-x-13-inch glass cake pan. Cool until somewhat thickened. Fold in:

> **1 15-ounce can crushed pineapple (in its own juice), drained (reserve juice)**
> **4 thinly sliced bananas**

Chill until firm. Make topping by combining in a saucepan:

> **1 cup reserved pineapple juice**
> **2 tablespoons flour**
> **¼ cup sugar**

Heat slowly, stirring constantly until smooth and thickened. Cool. Add:

> **1 cup nonfat whipped topping**

Spread entire mixture over gelatin. Chill for an hour or more before serving.

Variations: Any flavor of gelatin works well, including sugar-free. Add leftover fruit, or stir in juice instead of water.

Tips: Top with ½ cup low-fat cheddar cheese, if desired.

Nutritional Data for One Serving (1 large square): Calories: 178, Calories from Fat: 3, Total Fat: 0 g, Saturated Fat: 0 g, Cholesterol: 0 mg, Sodium: 58 mg, Total Carbohydrate: 44 g, Dietary Fiber: 1 g, Sugars: 37 g, Protein: 3 g, Vitamin A: 1% RDA, Vitamin C: 15% RDA, Calcium: 2% RDA, Iron: 2% RDA

Maple Waldorf Fruit Salad

From *Healthy Exchanges Food Newsletter.* *

2 cups unpeeled apples (4 small), cored and diced
1 cup diced bananas (1 medium)
¼ cup raisins
1 cup chopped celery
½ cup Kraft fat-free mayonnaise
¼ cup Cary's reduced-calorie maple syrup
¼ cup Peter Pan reduced-fat peanut butter

In a medium bowl, combine apples, bananas, raisins, and celery. In a small bowl, combine mayonnaise, maple syrup, and peanut butter. Mix well until smooth. Add mayonnaise mixture to apple mixture. Toss gently to combine. Cover and refrigerate until ready to serve.

Serves 8 (½ cup)
Each serving equals:
HE: 1 Fruit, ¼ Fat, ¼ Protein, 15 Optional Calories
118 Calories, 3 gm Fat, 2 gm Protein, 21 gm Carbohydrate, 164 mg Sodium, 2 gm Fiber
Diabetic: 1 Fruit, ½ Fat

HINT: To plump up raisins without "cooking," place in a glass measuring cup and microwave on HIGH for 20 seconds.

*Note: The format of this recipe differs from most others in this book at JoAnna Lund's—the author's—request that her original recipe remain exactly as it appeared in her newsletter.

Mashed Potatoes

Serves 8 to 10

Peel, then boil in lightly salted water, just enough to cover:

8 medium Russet potatoes

When potatoes are tender and break easily with a fork, drain. Mash. Beat in:

½ **cup nonfat yogurt**
¼ **cup skim milk**
¼ **cup parsley, finely chopped**
1 teaspoon onion powder
1 teaspoon salt
¼ **teaspoon black pepper**

Blend well, until potatoes are creamy. Serve with low-fat gravy (see Recipe Index).

Variations: Spices are entirely up to you; I wrote down the combination I like.

Tips: Until this year, I've never had any luck making lump-free mashed potatoes. My friend JoAnn tells me the secret is to boil the potatoes just long enough that they flake easily, but not so long that the cooking water clouds and potatoes are gluelike. Watch carefully and check often, and your potatoes will be perfect.

Nutritional Data for One Serving (about ⅔ cup): Calories: 114, Calories from Fat: 2, Total Fat: 0 g, Saturated Fat: 0 g, Cholesterol: 0 mg, Sodium: 257 mg, Total Carbohydrate: 26 g, Dietary Fiber: 2 g, Sugars: 3 g, Protein: 3 g, Vitamin A: 1% RDA, Vitamin C: 19% RDA, Calcium: 5% RDA, Iron: 3% RDA

Pasta Salad

Serves 8 to 10

Following package directions, prepare:

1 12-ounce package colored spiral pasta

Drain and pour into a large bowl. Add:

3 cups fresh vegetables, chopped
1 green bell pepper, chopped
2 tablespoons fresh parsley, chopped

Pour on just enough:

Nonfat Italian salad dressing

to lightly moisten vegetables. Toss gently.

Variations: Choose any fresh veggies you like.
Tips: To make this dish healthier, use vegetable pasta.

Nutritional Data for One Serving (about ½ cup): Calories: 169, Calories from Fat: 5, Total Fat: 1 g, Saturated Fat: 0 g, Cholesterol: 0 mg, Sodium: 217 mg, Total Carbohydrate: 35 g, Dietary Fiber: 3 g, Sugars: 3 g, Protein: 6 g, Vitamin A: 72% RDA, Vitamin C: 66% RDA, Calcium: 3% RDA, Iron: 13% RDA

Potato Chowder

Serves 8 to 10 *"who are very, very hungry"*

Adapted from a recipe in *A Taste of Dutch,* a cookbook by Jan Kent.

In a large Dutch oven or kettle, combine:

4 cups peeled, diced potatoes
1 cup grated carrot
½ cup finely chopped onion
1 tablespoon parsley flakes
1 teaspoon salt
¼ teaspoon pepper
4 chicken bouillon cubes (or equivalent broth powder)

Cover with water 1 inch above vegetables. Cook until tender, about 15 to 20 minutes. Do not drain. In a separate pan, scald:

6 cups skim milk

Heat until tiny bubbles form around the edge of the pan. Remove 1½ cups milk, then add:

2 tablespoons butter
½ cup flour

to 1½ cups hot milk. Stir with a wire whisk until smooth. Add remaining hot milk to undrained vegetables, then stir in thickened milk. Blend well. Simmer for 15 minutes on low heat.

Variations: Add bits of leftover veggies, diced meat, or imitation crab for a seafood delight.

Tips: Jan suggests serving this chowder with whole-wheat bread.

Nutritional Data for One Serving (a big bowl): Calories: 202, Calories from Fat: 28, Total Fat: 3 g, Saturated Fat: 2 g, Cholesterol: 10 mg, Sodium: 871 mg, Total Carbohydrate: 35 g, Dietary Fiber: 3 g, Sugars: 8 g, Protein: 9 g, Vitamin A: 47% RDA, Vitamin C: 39% RDA, Calcium: 22% RDA, Iron: 8% RDA

Refried Beans

Makes about 4 cups

Drain:

4 cups cooked Basic Beans (see Recipe Index)

Reserve:

1 cup liquid

In a large nonstick skillet, heat beans and liquid over medium heat. Mash beans until smooth. Continue cooking, stirring constantly, about 5 minutes, or until beans thicken.

Nutritional Data for One Serving (½ cup): Calories: 118, Calories from Fat: 5, Total Fat: 1 g, Saturated Fat: 0 g, Cholesterol: 0 mg, Sodium: 413 mg, Total Carbohydrate: 58 g, Dietary Fiber: 7 g, Sugars: 4 g, Protein: 8 g, Vitamin A: 4% RDA, Vitamin C: 14% RDA, Calcium: 6% RDA, Iron: 17% RDA

Scalloped Potatoes

Serves 6

Preheat oven to 325 degrees. Coat a 3-quart casserole dish with non-fat cooking spray; set aside. Thinly slice:

4 cups potatoes
1 large onion

Place one-third of the potatoes and onions in the casserole dish. Dot with:

1 teaspoon reduced-calorie margarine

Repeat with two more layers, and 2 (more) teaspoons reduced calorie margarine, 1 teaspoon for each layer. Set aside. In a quart jar, place:

6 tablespoons flour
½ cup dry milk
1 teaspoon salt
¼ teaspoon pepper

Seal and shake thoroughly. Add to jar:

3 cups skim milk

Reseal and shake until all flour is dissolved. Pour milk mixture over potato mixture. Add enough milk to cover potatoes, if needed. Bake for 1½ hours, until potatoes break easily with a fork.

Variations and Tips: For Potato-Lentil Casserole, substitute 1 cup lentils for half of the potatoes and increase the milk to 3½ cups. For Au Gratin Potatoes, add 1½ to 2 cups cubed cheese (choose a lower-fat variety) to the Scalloped Potatoes recipe.

Nutritional Data for One Serving (about ⅔ cup): Calories: 238, Calories from Fat: 15, Total Fat: 2 g, Saturated Fat: 0 g, Cholesterol: 3 mg, Sodium: 482 mg, Total Carbohydrate: 46 g, Dietary Fiber: 3 g, Sugars: 6 g, Protein: 11 g, Vitamin A: 14% RDA, Vitamin C: 56% RDA, Calcium: 24% RDA, Iron: 9% RDA

Stuffed Potatoes

Serves as many as needed

Scrub potatoes with a brush and water until clean. Cook, either in the oven or in the microwave, until potato feels soft when pressed between two fingers covered with a hot pad. Cooking time in the oven is about 40 to 60 minutes at 425 degrees, or 60 to 80 minutes at 375 degrees (if you're already baking something else at that temperature). Microwave time varies significantly: plan on 10 to 15 minutes.

Top potatoes with one of the following combinations:

Chili (see Recipe Index) and reduced-fat, grated cheese
Taco meat, shredded lettuce, diced tomatoes, black olives, grated reduced-fat cheese, low-fat sour cream

Steamed broccoli spears and reduced-fat cheddar
Zucchini slices, diced tomatoes, diced onions, basil, salt
and pepper, and part-skim mozzarella cheese
Pizza sauce, Italian seasonings, and part-skim mozzarella
cheese
Cooked, diced ham and shredded cheese

Variations and Tips: My mother's variation of this recipe was Twice-Baked Potatoes: Cook potatoes as above. Cool. Hollow out potato skins and make mashed potatoes. Refill skins with mashed potatoes. Top with low-fat cheese. Bake or microwave until potatoes are reheated.

Nutritional Data for One Serving: Too hard to figure, with all these options.

Stuffing

Serves 8

Adapted from a recipe in *Cheap Eating,* by Pat Edwards.

Combine in a 1-quart saucepan:

1 tablespoon reduced-fat margarine, melted
1 onion, finely chopped

Add:

2 teaspoons sage
2 cloves garlic (or 2 teaspoons garlic powder)

Mix well. Lightly toss in:

8 cups dried bread cubes

Add:

4 cups defatted chicken broth or prepared bouillon

Bread may seem to melt but should hold its form. Use to stuff a turkey or chicken, or bake in a casserole dish coated with nonstick cooking spray for 35 to 40 minutes at 350 degrees.

Variations: Add ½ to 1 cup chopped celery, 1½ cups sliced mushrooms, 1 cup cooked poultry, or ½ cup raisins to stuffing.

Tips: Make your own bread cubes from leftover bread ends and pieces you've collected in your freezer, rather than buying the prepackaged kind.

Nutritional Data for One Serving (1 cup): Calories: 116, Calories from Fat: 24, Total Fat: 3 g, Saturated Fat: 1 g, Cholesterol: 1 mg, Sodium: 559 mg, Total Carbohydrate: 17 g, Dietary Fiber: 1 g, Sugars: 2 g, Protein: 5 g, Vitamin A: 2% RDA, Vitamin C: 2% RDA, Calcium: 5% RDA, Iron: 7% RDA

Whole-Wheat Pasta

Serves 6

Combine in a large bowl:

2 cups whole-wheat flour
1 cup white flour
¾ cup water
2 egg whites, beaten well
1 tablespoon canola or olive oil
½ teaspoon salt

Knead until dough forms a ball and feels smooth. Add a little more water if needed. Dough should be stiff but manageable. Lay out, covered, on a floured surface. Let rest for 10 minutes.

To make noodles, divide dough in half. Roll out one piece to about ¹⁄₁₆-inch thickness, turning often and adding flour as needed. Roll up lightly into a cylinder. Cut into strips, whatever size you like (about ⅛ to ¼ inch for noodles, for example). Unroll noodles; place on a cookie sheet to dry. Repeat the process with the second half of the dough. To cook pasta, in a large saucepan, bring to a boil:

8 cups water
1 teaspoon salt

Add pasta. Cook from 5 to 10 minutes, until pasta is tender. Drain.

Variations: Use a food processor or heavy-duty mixer to prepare the dough.

Tips: This pasta takes time, but the taste and nutrition are worth it.

Nutritional Data for One Serving (about ⅔ cup cooked noodles): Calories: 244, Calories from Fat: 30, Total Fat: 3 g, Saturated Fat: 0 g, Cholesterol: 0 mg, Sodium: 199 mg, Total Carbohydrate: 46 g, Dietary Fiber: 6 g, Sugars: 1 g, Protein: 9 g, Vitamin A: 0% RDA, Vitamin C: 0% RDA, Calcium: 2% RDA, Iron: 13% RDA

MISCELLANEOUS

Dragon Sauce

Makes a little more than 3 cups

Adapted from a recipe in *Dinner's in the Freezer,* by Jill Bond.

In a saucepan, evenly mix:

3 cups peach nectar
3 tablespoons cornstarch

Make sure lumps are all gone. Add:

¼ cup fructose (or ½ cup sugar)
¼ cup vinegar
1 to 2 tablespoons soy sauce

Cook over medium heat until thick and transparent, about 10 minutes.

Variations and Tips: Jill says, "I like to buy the #10 can of peaches, make a cobbler with the peaches, and use the syrup for this sauce. To make it extra rich, save out some of the peaches, blend them until they're semi-liquid with small peach pieces visible. Add these pureed peaches to the sauce. This goes well with egg rolls, over chicken and duckling. It's even delicious over rice." Use more cornstarch for a thicker sauce, less for a thinner one. Substitute pineapple, apricot, and/or plum juice/syrup for peach nectar.

Nutritional Data for One Serving (¼ cup): Calories: 75, Calories from Fat: 0, Total Fat: 0 g, Saturated Fat: 0 g, Cholesterol: 0 mg, Sodium: 133 mg, Total Carbohydrate: 19 g, Dietary Fiber: 0 g, Sugars: 8 g, Protein: 0 g, Vitamin A: 2% RDA, Vitamin C: 5% RDA, Calcium: 0% RDA, Iron: 1% RDA

Drinks

Here are some quick, easy ideas for drinks. For more suggestions, see Chapter 3 under "Make or Cook Your Own: Drinks."

Diet Hot Chocolate

Mix together in a large cup:

> ½ **cup dry milk powder**
> **1 teaspoon cocoa**
> **Sweetener equivalent to 2 teaspoons sugar**
> **Enough boiling (or very hot) water to fill cup**

Mix thoroughly. Top with marshmallows, if desired.

Abbreviated Nutritional Data (per cup): 129 Calories, 0 Fat, 19 g Carbohydrate, 0 Sugar, 13 g Protein.

Florida Cracker Lemonade

From a recipe in *Dinner's in the Freezer,* by Jill Bond.

Place in very hot water for 10 minutes, or microwave for 30 seconds:

Several lemons

Juice. Heat the juice in a small saucepan, adding:

1 teaspoon fructose (or 2 teaspoons sugar)

per lemon juiced. Stir until dissolved. In a pitcher, add juice mixture to:

2 cups water

per lemon used. Slice a lemon very thinly and float rings in the juice.

Abbreviated Nutritional Data (per glass): 27 Calories, 0 Fat, 10 g Carbohydrate, 5 g Sugars.

Smoothie

Combine in a blender:

1½ cups skim milk
1 large diced banana
1 tablespoon honey
1 teaspoon vanilla

Blend until smooth (hence, the name).

Abbreviated Nutritional Data (2-cup serving, a large milkshake glass): 313 Calories, 1 g Fat, 63 g Carbohydrate, 51 g Sugars, 14 g Protein.

Sun Tea

Fill a half-gallon glass jar with water. Add three teabags of your favorite brand of tea. Cover loosely. Set out in the sun. Brewed tea will be ready in a few hours.

Low-Fat French Salad Dressing

Makes about 3 cups

Combine in a blender:

¾ cup sugar
½ cup vinegar
½ cup ketchup
1 teaspoon celery seed
1 teaspoon paprika
1 teaspoon salt
1 teaspoon onion powder

Mix together thoroughly.

Variations: Finely chopped onions can substitute for onion juice.
I have also used other kinds of seeds, such as dill, instead of celery.
You can try whatever spices you have on hand.

Tips: Store in the refrigerator in a tightly covered jar. Shake well
before serving.

Nutritional Data for One Serving (2 tablespoons): Calories: 31, Calories from Fat: 0 g, Total
Fat: 0 g, Saturated Fat: 0 g, Cholesterol: 0 mg, Sodium: 157 mg, Total Carbohydrate: 8 g, Dietary Fiber:
0 g, Sugars: 7 g, Protein: 0 g, Vitamin A: 1% RDA, Vitamin C: 2% RDA, Calcium: 0% RDA, Iron: 1% RDA

Low-Fat Ranch Salad Dressing

Makes 2 cups

Combine in a blender:

1 cup reduced-fat mayonnaise
1 cup buttermilk (see Milk Substitutes, following)
2 tablespoons onion juice
2 teaspoons parsley, finely chopped
¼ teaspoon salt
¼ teaspoon garlic powder
¼ teaspoon paprika
¼ teaspoon black pepper

Mix well. Store covered in the refrigerator.

Variations: Add more or less spice according to your taste. Substitute plain yogurt for mayonnaise. I sometimes use 2 tablespoons of onion powder in place of onion juice.

Tips: These two salad dressings are much cheaper than store-bought, nutritious and delicious.

Nutritional Data for One Serving (2 tablespoons): Calories: 47, Calories from Fat: 37, Total Fat: 4 g, Saturated Fat: 1 g, Cholesterol: 6 mg, Sodium: 65 mg, Total Carbohydrate: 2 g, Dietary Fiber: 0 g, Sugars: 1 g, Protein: 1 g, Vitamin A: 1% RDA, Vitamin C: 1% RDA, Calcium: 2% RDA, Iron: 0% RDA

Milk Substitutes and Products

Low-Fat Sour Cream

Combine in a blender:

1 cup low-fat cottage cheese
1 tablespoon skim milk
2 tablespoons lemon juice

Blend until smooth.

Tips: You can also substitute 1 cup nonfat yogurt for 1 cup sour cream in many recipes.

Nutritional Data for One Serving (1 tablespoon): Calories: 13, Calories from Fat: 3, Total Fat: 0 g, Saturated Fat: 0 g, Cholesterol: 1 mg, Sodium: 58 mg, Total Carbohydrate: 1 g, Dietary Fiber: 0 g, Sugars: 1 g, Protein: 2 g, Vitamin A: 0% RDA, Vitamin C: 1% RDA, Calcium: 1% RDA, Iron: 0% RDA

Soured Milk or Buttermilk

Place in an empty 1 cup container:

1 tablespoon lemon juice

Fill to the top with:

Skim milk

Tips: Use in place of 1 cup buttermilk or 1 cup soured milk.

Sweetened Condensed Milk

Mix in a blender until thickened:

1 cup dry nonfat milk powder
½ cup boiling water
⅔ cup sugar
3 tablespoons reduced-fat margarine, melted
Pinch of salt

Store in a tightly covered container in the refrigerator.

Tips: This recipe yields the same amount as 1 can of Eagle Brand milk and can be used in any recipe calling for it.

Nutritional Data for One Serving (1 tablespoon): Calories: 13, Calories from Fat: 3, Total Fat: 0 g, Saturated Fat: 0 g, Cholesterol: 1 mg, Sodium: 58 mg, Total Carbohydrate: 1 g, Dietary Fiber: 0 g, Sugars: 1 g, Protein: 2 g, Vitamin A: 0% RDA, Vitamin C: 1% RDA, Calcium: 1% RDA, Iron: 0% RDA

Whipped Topping

Makes about 2 cups

Combine in a shallow, chilled bowl:

1 cup icy cold water
1 teaspoon lemon juice
1 package unflavored gelatin
Pinch of cream of tartar

With chilled beaters, blend in:

1 cup nonfat dry milk powder

Whip at high speed until light and fluffy, with soft peaks forming. Continue to beat, adding:

⅓ cup sugar
½ teaspoon vanilla

Serve at once, or chill.

Variations: Add a touch of cinnamon or a little more (or less) lemon juice, as you prefer.

Tips: You can cut down on the amount of time needed for whipping if you set the cold water in a metal bowl in the freezer, just until ice crystals start to form. The taste of this topping is delicious, though the consistency is more liquid than that of the store-bought version. You may need to beat the mixture for several minutes.

Nutritional Data for One Serving (2 tablespoons): Calories: 33, Calories from Fat: 0, Total Fat: 0 g, Saturated Fat: 0 g, Cholesterol: 1 mg, Sodium: 24 mg, Total Carbohydrate: 6 g, Dietary Fiber: 0 g, Sugars: 4 g, Protein: 2 g, Vitamin A: 3% RDA, Vitamin C: 1% RDA, Calcium: 5% RDA, Iron: 0% RDA

Yogurt

Makes about 8 cups

Preheat oven to 200 degrees. Heat in a large saucepan:

2 quarts (8 cups) milk

Use candy thermometer to gauge when milk reaches 180 degrees. Remove from heat and cool to 112 degrees. Measure ¾ cup hot milk into a small pan. Stir into this smaller amount of milk:

4 to 6 tablespoons plain yogurt

one tablespoon at a time, mixing thoroughly each time. Pour ¾ cup milk and blended yogurt back into saucepan. Stir until well mixed. Reheat to 112 degrees if temperature has dropped. Pour into hot, sterilized jars; place yogurt-filled jars in a cake pan. Turn preheated oven off. Put cake pan into warm oven. Turn on oven light and leave jars in oven overnight. Yogurt will be ready in the morning.

Variations: Once yogurt is set, blend in any mixture of fruit, syrup, or juice you like.

Tips: If you have a yogurt maker, follow the manufacturer's directions and the above recipe. It's best to use whole or 2% milk rather than skim. New yogurt can be made from 4 to 6 tablespoons of your plain yogurt (providing the yogurt is no older than 4 to 5 days). Use yogurt in place of mayonnaise or sour cream in most recipes. (You can even make your own "cream cheese," below.)

Nutritional Data for One Serving (1 cup): Calories: 130, Calories from Fat: 45, Total Fat: 5 g, Saturated Fat: 3 g, Cholesterol: 19 mg, Sodium: 129 mg, Total Carbohydrate: 12 g, Dietary Fiber: 0 g, Sugars: 12 g, Protein: 9 g, Vitamin A: 15% RDA, Vitamin C: 4% RDA, Calcium: 32% RDA, Iron: 1% RDA

Yogurt Cream Cheese

Stir plain unflavored yogurt and pour off liquid whey. Place a colander over a pan, and in the colander layer three large folds of cheesecloth. Empty yogurt onto cheesecloth layers so that liquid drains into pan below. Tie up ends of cheesecloth into a loose knot. Drain yogurt for 8 hours (or overnight). Yogurt cheese should have the same consistency as cream cheese, but with a tangier taste.

DESSERTS

Apple Crisp

Serves 8 to 10

Preheat oven to 375 degrees. Peel and slice:

3 to 5 pounds apples

Coat a large cake pan with nonstick cooking spray. Place apple slices in pan and sprinkle with:
3 tablespoons sugar
2 teaspoons cinnamon

Set aside. In a medium-size bowl, combine:

1 cup whole-wheat flour
1 cup brown sugar
½ cup rolled oats
⅓ cup melted low-fat or nonfat margarine

Mix well, until crumbly. Spoon over apples. Bake for 35 minutes, or until apples are tender and bubbly.

Variations: If apples are tart, sprinkle on more sugar. Substitute any seasonal fruit you like.

Tips: Serve hot or cold, plain or with low-fat whipped topping.

Nutritional Data for One Serving (about ¾ cup): Calories: 317, Calories from Fat: 41, Total Fat: 5 g, Saturated Fat: 1 g, Cholesterol: 0 mg, Sodium: 87 mg, Total Carbohydrate: 71 g, Dietary Fiber: 5 g, Sugars: 30 g, Protein: 3 g, Vitamin A: 9% RDA, Vitamin C: 14% RDA, Calcium: 4% RDA, Iron: 8% RDA

Applesauce Gingerbread

Serves 16

From a recipe in *Secrets of Fat-Free Baking,* by Sandra Woodruff.

Preheat oven to 325 degrees. Combine:

**1 ½ cups unbleached flour
1 cup whole-wheat flour
⅔ cup sugar
2½ teaspoons baking soda
1 teaspoon ground ginger
1 teaspoon ground cinnamon
1 teaspoon ground allspice**

Stir to mix well. Add:

**1½ cups unsweetened applesauce
1 cup molasses
3 egg whites**

Stir to mix well. Coat a 9-x-13-inch pan with nonstick cooking spray. Spread the batter evenly in the pan, and bake at 325 degrees for 40 minutes, or just until a wooden toothpick inserted in the center of the cake comes out clean. Cool the cake for at least 20 minutes. Cut into squares and serve warm or at room temperature with a light whipped topping, if desired.

Variations (my own idea): Substitute 3 teaspoons apple pie spice for ginger, cinnamon, and allspice.
Tips: The texture of low-fat cakes is different from that of "normal" cakes. Be prepared for more chewiness.

Nutritional Data for One Serving (1 square): Calories: 157, Total Fat: 0.3 g, Protein: 3.1 g, Cholesterol: 0 g, Sodium: 146 mg, Fiber: 1.6 g, Calcium: 38 mg, Potassium: 255 mg

Baked Apples

Serves 6

Preheat oven to 400 degrees. Core, leaving ½ inch from the bottom intact:

6 medium apples

Measure out:

6 teaspoons raisins
6 teaspoons all-fruit spread, any flavor

Fill each cored apple with 1 teaspoon raisins, then 1 teaspoon spread. Coat baking dish with nonstick cooking spray. Place apples in baking dish. Cover with foil. Bake for 25 to 30 minutes, until apples are tender.

Variations: Fill the centers with all-fruit spread and a little maple syrup, omitting raisins. Or peel and cut up apples, spooning fruit spread and raisins over the top.

Nutritional Data for One Serving (1 apple): Calories: 97, Calories from Fat: 6, Total Fat: 1 g, Saturated Fat: 0 g, Cholesterol: 0 mg, Sodium: 6 mg, Total Carbohydrate: 25 g, Dietary Fiber: 3 g, Sugars: 20 g, Protein: 0 g, Vitamin A: 1% RDA, Vitamin C: 13% RDA, Calcium: 1% RDA, Iron: 2% RDA

Baked Custard

Serves 8 to 10

Preheat oven to 350 degrees. In a large saucepan, scald until nearly boiling:

4½ cups skim milk

Combine in a large bowl:

1 cup egg whites
¾ cup honey
½ teaspoon salt

Pour into scalded milk. Add:

1 teaspoon vanilla

Blend well. Pour custard into a large ovenproof casserole dish and place the dish in a baking pan filled with 1 inch of water. Set in oven. Bake for 50 to 60 minutes, or until knife inserted in center comes out clean.

Variations: Sprinkle with a little cinnamon just before baking. The 2% milk makes a firmer custard; don't use reconstituted nonfat dry milk in this recipe.

Tips: This low-fat, nutritious dessert is truly delicious. Serve hot or well chilled, as you like it.

Nutritional Data for One Serving (½ to ¾ cup): Calories: 137, Calories from Fat: 2, Total Fat: 0 g, Saturated Fat: 0 g, Cholesterol: 2 mg, Sodium: 207 mg, Total Carbohydrate: 29 g, Dietary Fiber: 0 g, Sugars: 5 g, Protein: 6 g, Vitamin A: 7% RDA, Vitamin C: 2% RDA, Calcium: 15% RDA, Iron: 1% RDA

Bread Pudding

Serves 6

Preheat oven to 350 degrees. Coat a 2-quart casserole dish with non-stick cooking spray. Combine in the casserole dish:

8 slices whole-wheat bread, crusts trimmed, cubed
1 12-ounce can evaporated skim milk

Let stand for 10 minutes. Stir in:

½ cup raisins

Set aside. In a small bowl, beat together :

3 egg whites
1 whole egg
1 cup skim milk
½ cup brown sugar
1 teaspoon vanilla
½ teaspoon cinnamon

Pour over bread mixture. Bake for 45 to 50 minutes.

Variations: Leave out raisins. Serve hot with whipped topping.
Tips: Save the trimmed bread crusts and make them into croutons or bread sticks (see Recipe Index).

Nutritional Data for One Serving (about ¾ cup): Calories: 281, Calories from Fat: 24, Total Fat: 3 g, Saturated Fat: 1 g, Cholesterol: 38 mg, Sodium: 331 mg, Total Carbohydrate: 54 g, Dietary Fiber: 1 g, Sugars: 10 g, Protein: 12 g, Vitamin A: 11% RDA, Vitamin C: 17% RDA, Calcium: 27% RDA, Iron: 12% RDA

Caramel Apricot Rice Pudding

From *Healthy Exchanges Food Newsletter.* *

2 cups water
1 cup diced dried apricots (4½ ounces)
1⅓ cups dry instant Minute Rice (4 ounces)
1 (4 serving) package Jell-O sugar-free instant
butterscotch pudding mix
⅔ cup Carnation nonfat dry milk powder
1½ cups water
¼ cup Cool Whip Lite
1 teaspoon vanilla extract

In a medium saucepan, combine water and diced apricots. Bring mixture to a boil. Remove from heat. Stir in dry rice. Cover. Let set 15 minutes to cool. In a large bowl, combine dry pudding mix and dry milk powder. Add water. Mix well using a wire whisk. Blend in Cool Whip Lite and vanilla extract. Fold in cooled rice mixture. Mix gently to combine. Evenly spoon mixture into 6 dessert dishes. Refrigerate until ready to serve. Freezes well.

Serves 6
Each serving equals:
HE: 1 Fruit, ⅔ Bread, ⅓ Skim Milk, ¼ Slider, 2 Optional Calories
140 Calories, 0 gm Fat, 4 gm Protein, 31 gm Carbohydrate, 264 mg Sodium, 2 gm Fiber
Diabetic: 1 Fat, ½ Starch, ½ Skim Milk

*Note: The format of this recipe differs from most others in this book at JoAnna Lund's—the author's—request that her original recipe remain exactly as it appeared in her newsletter.

Caramel Corn

Serves 24

Preheat oven to 250 degrees. Prepare in a popcorn popper:

12 quarts (3 very large bowls, or 48 cups) air-popped corn

Set aside. Combine in a large, heavy-duty saucepan:

2 cups brown sugar
1½ sticks low-fat margarine
½ cup white syrup
¼ teaspoon cream of tartar
¼ teaspoon salt

Bring to a rolling boil. Let boil, stirring occasionally, for 5 minutes. Remove from heat. Add:

1½ teaspoons baking soda

Mix well. Working fast, stir hot caramel mixture into popped corn until thoroughly blended. Spread on cookie sheets coated with non-stick cooking spray. Bake for 30 minutes, stirring once or twice. Remove from oven. When lukewarm, break into small pieces. Cool completely. Store in airtight containers.

Variations: The original recipe makes a very rich candy, as the syrup is spread over 6 quarts of popped corn. (Sometimes I make a small batch like this for our neighbors as a special treat.)

Tips: If the syrup cools before you are able to spread it all on the popcorn, reheat briefly on the stove. Caramel corn can be stored in the freezer for several months or in the refrigerator for a few weeks. This is one of my children's favorite treats.

Nutritional Data for One Serving (2 cups): Calories: 193, Calories from Fat: 38, Total Fat: 4 g, Saturated Fat: 1 g, Cholesterol: 0 mg, Sodium: 136 mg, Total Carbohydrate: 39 g, Dietary Fiber: 2 g, Sugars: 5 g, Protein: 3 g, Vitamin A: 8% RDA, Vitamin C: 0% RDA, Calcium: 2% RDA, Iron: 5% RDA

Chocolate Tortilla Torte

Serves 6

Pour into a medium-size bowl:

1 cup skim milk
1 (4-serving size) package chocolate sugar-free instant pudding mix
¼ teaspoon cinnamon

Beat for 2 minutes with wire whisk. Gently stir in, until well-blended:

½ cup whipped topping

Lay out:

5 (5- to 6-inch) flour tortillas

Spread about ¼ cup pudding mixture on 1 flour tortilla. Repeat layers, ending with pudding mixture. Refrigerate, lightly covered, for 2 to 3 hours. Garnish with a dollop of whipped topping.

Variations: I usually prepare this recipe the night after I've served pudding for dessert and saved back some leftover pudding. Instead of pudding, combine whipped topping with all-fruit spread.

Tips: Garnish with chocolate syrup (cocoa and sugar mixed with a little hot water).

Nutritional Data for One Serving (1 generous wedge): Calories: 128, Calories from Fat: 19, Total Fat: 2 g, Saturated Fat: 0 g, Cholesterol: 1mg, Sodium: 170 mg, Total Carbohydrate: 22 g, Dietary Fiber: 0 g, Sugars: 2 g, Protein: 4 g, Vitamin A: 2% RDA, Vitamin C: 1% RDA, Calcium: 10% RDA, Iron: 7% RDA

Crystallized Grapes and Oranges

Serves 4

Adapted from a recipe in *Cheap Eating,* by Pat Edwards.

In a small bowl, lightly beat until foamy:

1 egg white

Roll in egg white:

3 cups seedless grapes
2 oranges or tangerines, cut into wedges

Immediately roll coated fruit in:

1 cup sugar

Let dry and serve.

Variations: Try a variety of grapes. Pat likes to serve this showy dessert for holidays.

Tips: If you're surprised at how high in both sugar and calories this recipe is, it's because the nutritional analyst estimated ¼ cup sugar per serving (just as the recipe says). You can actually get by with much less sugar by very lightly rolling the fruit in it.

Nutritional Data for One Serving (1¼ cups): Calories: 273, Calories from Fat: 3, Total Fat: 0 g, Saturated Fat: 0 g, Cholesterol: 0 mg, Sodium: 17 mg, Total Carbohydrate: 70 g, Dietary Fiber: 6 g, Sugars: 70 g, Protein: 2 g, Vitamin A: 1% RDA, Vitamin C: 99% RDA, Calcium: 5% RDA, Iron: 2% RDA

Five-Minute Chocolate Custard Pie

Serves 6 to 8

Preheat oven to 350 degrees. Combine in a blender:

2 cups skim milk
8 egg whites
⅔ cup sugar
½ cup flour
⅓ cup cocoa, sifted
1 teaspoon vanilla
Pinch of salt

Set aside. Use:

1 teaspoon low-fat margarine, melted
2 tablespoons flour

to coat and flour two 8-inch pie pans or ovenproof casserole dishes.
Blend milk/egg mixture a few seconds, until smooth. Pour into pans
or dishes. Bake for 30 minutes, or until knife inserted in center comes
out clean.

Variations: Omit cocoa and add 2 teaspoons cinnamon.
Tips: This recipe actually takes me 5 minutes to assemble, and it
even makes its own crust. We like the pie best when it's chilled for 2
hours or more before serving, but you can also serve it hot.

Nutritional Data for One Serving (1 large slice): Calories: 161, Calories from Fat: 5, Total
Fat: 1 g, Saturated Fat: 0 g, Cholesterol: 1 mg, Sodium: 151 mg, Total Carbohydrate: 31 g, Dietary
Fiber: 0 g, Sugars: 22 g, Protein: 7 g, Vitamin A: 7% RDA, Vitamin C: 3% RDA, Calcium: 9% RDA, Iron:
3% RDA

Fudge Brownies

Serves 36 (small squares)

Adapted from "Very Best Fudge Brownies," in
Secrets of Fat Free Baking, by Sandra Woodruff.

Preheat oven to 325 degrees. Melt:

4 (1-ounce) squares unsweetened baking chocolate

If using a microwave oven to melt chocolate, place the chocolate in a
mixing bowl and microwave uncovered at high power for 3 to 4 minutes, or until almost melted. Remove the bowl from the microwave
and stir the chocolate until completely melted. If melting the chocolate on a stovetop, place the chocolate in a small saucepan and cook
over low heat, stirring constantly, until melted. Add to the chocolate:

1½ cups sugar
½ cup + 1 tablespoon fat-free egg substitute
¾ cup prune butter (see below)
2 teaspoons vanilla

Stir to mix well. Stir in:

1 cup unbleached flour

Coat a 9-x-13-inch pan with nonstick cooking spray. Spread the batter
evenly in the pan, and bake for 35 to 40 minutes, or until edges are
firm and the center is almost set. Cool to room temperature, cut into
squares, and serve.

    Variations: When I tried this recipe, I used fresh pumpkin puree
in place of prune butter; canned pumpkin works, too. Optional ingredients in this recipe include ¼ teaspoon salt and ¾ cup chopped
walnuts.
    Tips: If you're making a cut-up party cake, this recipe works well,
as the brownie mixture slices better than most cakes.

Nutritional Data Per Serving (1 small square, without optional ingredients): Calories:
74, Fiber: 1.1 g, Fat: 1.7 g, Calcium: 6 mg, Protein: 1.3 g, Potassium: 72 mg, Cholesterol: 0 mg, Iron:
0.6 mg, Sodium: 21 mg

Gelatin Desserts

Here are some ideas for quick, healthy gelatin desserts.

Diet Gelatin

Serves 4

Mix together in a small saucepan:

½ can of fruit-flavored diet soda
1 package plain gelatin

Bring to a boil, stirring constantly. Mix well. Remove from heat. Add:

(Other) ½ can of fruit-flavored diet soda

Stir until completely dissolved. Chill until set.

Juice Gelatin

Follow the Diet Gelatin recipe, but substitute juice (orange, grape, apple, cherry; anything but pineapple) in place of diet soda.

Variations: Make a vegetable gelatin with grated carrots and finely diced celery. Add apples, raisins, and nuts. Mash overly ripe bananas and blend into gelatin. Use up excess juice from canned fruits. This is the perfect place to "recycle" some carefully selected leftovers.

Tips: Make sure gelatin is completely dissolved in hot liquid before adding cold liquid.

Nutritional Data for One Serving: Too many variables to tell.

Ice Pops

Gelatin Pops

Prepare your favorite gelatin recipe (see Recipe Index, or follow directions on a store-bought box, regular or sugar-free). Use 1½ times the water called for in the recipe. Pour into pop molds and freeze.

Pudding Pops

Make the recipe for homemade pudding that follows, but use 1½ times the milk (a mixture of reconstituted dry and skim, or all skim) required. Mix well. Pour into ice pop molds and freeze.

Yogurt Pops

Combine:
2 cups plain nonfat yogurt
1 cup juice (apple, grape, orange, etc.)
1 tablespoon honey
1 teaspoon vanilla

Beat with a whisk until smooth. Pour into ice pop molds and freeze.

Variations: Puree overly ripe bananas and add to ice pops. Use up leftover fruit juice, nectar, bits of fruit, or "flopped" puddings or yogurt. Alternate a layer of gelatin mixture with a different-colored layer, perhaps some all-fruit spread. Shake milk in a jelly jar that's nearly empty, mixing the last of the jelly with the milk. Etc., etc.

Tips: If you don't have ice pop molds and can't find any at yard sales, pour above mixtures into little paper cups, freeze for an hour, then insert wooden sticks into the partially set mixture. Or pour the mixture into metal baking pans, making a thin layer, and freeze (grown-ups will probably prefer a "slush" rather than a "pop").

Nutritional Data for One Serving: Too hard to figure with all the variations.

Impossible Pumpkin Pie

Serves 6

Preheat oven to 350 degrees. Coat a 9-inch pie pan with nonstick cooking spray and lightly flour. Combine in a blender:

1 16-ounce can pumpkin
1 13-ounce can evaporated skim milk
4 egg whites
¾ cup sugar
½ cup flour
½ teaspoon baking powder
Pinch of salt
2½ teaspoons pumpkin pie spice
2 teaspoons vanilla
1 teaspoon melted butter

Blend well, about 1 minute in blender, or 2 minutes with hand beater. Pour into pie pan. Bake about 50 to 55 minutes, until knife inserted in center comes out clean.

Variations: Substitute ½ cup Bisquick baking mix for flour, baking powder, and salt.

Tips: This pie makes its own low-fat crust, and it's tasty.

Nutritional Data for One Serving (1 medium wedge): Calories: 240, Calories from Fat: 22, Total Fat: 2 g, Saturated Fat: 1 g, Cholesterol: 4 mg, Sodium: 244 mg, Total Carbohydrate: 46 g, Dietary Fiber: 2 g, Sugars: 25 g, Protein: 9 g, Vitamin A: 175% RDA, Vitamin C: 7% RDA, Calcium: 23% RDA, Iron: 8% RDA

Oatmeal Crispies

Makes 4 dozen or more

Preheat oven to 350 degrees. Combine in a large bowl:

1 cup sugar
1 cup brown sugar
⅔ cup applesauce
⅓ cup shortening
4 egg whites

Stir in:

> **1 cup whole-wheat flour**
> **1 cup white flour**
> **2 cups rolled oats**
> **1 teaspoon salt**
> **1 teaspoon baking soda**

Mix well. Drop by tablespoonsful onto cookie sheets coated lightly with nonstick cooking spray. Bake for 8 to 10 minutes, or until very lightly browned.

Variations: Add tiny chocolate chips or raisins to the dough. Use more flour for a puffier kind of cookie; these are thin and crisp.

Tips: My favorite cookies are the ones with mega-fat: this recipe, for example, originally called for 1 cup of shortening. I think these are the tastiest low-fat version I've tried.

Nutritional Data for One Serving (1 cookie): Calories: 81, Calories from Fat: 15, Total Fat: 2 g, Saturated Fat: 0 g, Cholesterol: 0 mg, Sodium: 77 mg, Total Carbohydrate: 15 g, Dietary Fiber: 1 g, Sugars: 5 g, Protein: 1 g, Vitamin A: 0% RDA, Vitamin C: 0% RDA, Calcium: 1% RDA, Iron: 2% RDA

Orange Sherbet

Makes 1½ quarts (about 12 servings)

Place in a small metal bowl, in the freezer:

> **1 can evaporated milk**

Leave in freezer just until ice crystals begin to form, about 30 minutes. Remove. Whip milk with an electric beater until stiff peaks form. Beat in:

> **6 ounces frozen orange juice concentrate, thawed**
> **⅓ cup sugar**

Return to freezer and freeze until firm, about 1 to 2 hours.

Variations: Try other juices instead of orange juice.

Tips: This is a really delicious, cheap, healthy recipe: what more could you ask for? I prefer to eat the sherbet when it's still the consistency of whipped cream, before it freezes solid.

Nutritional Data for One Serving (½ cup): Calories: 69, Calories from Fat: 1, Total Fat: 0 g, Saturated Fat: 0 g, Cholesterol: 1 mg, Sodium: 37 mg, Total Carbohydrate: 14 g, Dietary Fiber: 0 g, Sugars: 5 g, Protein: 3 g, Vitamin A: 4% RDA, Vitamin C: 37% RDA, Calcium: 10% RDA, Iron: 1% RDA

Pineapple Torte

From *Healthy Exchanges Food Newsletter.* *

1 cup canned crushed pineapple, packed in its own juice, drained, and reserve liquid (8-ounce can)
1 teaspoon lemon juice
1 (4 serving) package Jell-O sugar-free vanilla cook-and-serve pudding mix
⅔ cup Carnation nonfat dry milk powder
1 cup Cool Whip Lite
12 (2½-inch) graham crackers, crushed (¾ cup)

Add enough water to reserved pineapple juice to make 1 cup liquid. Pour liquid into medium saucepan. Add lemon juice, dry pudding mix, and dry milk powder. Mix well to combine. Cook over medium heat until mixture thickens and starts to boil, stirring constantly. Remove from heat. Stir in pineapple. Cool 30 minutes. Fold in Cool Whip Lite. Save 2 tablespoons graham cracker crumbs. Spread remaining crumbs in an 8-x-8-inch dish sprayed with butter-flavored cooking spray. Pour pineapple mixture evenly over crumbs. Sprinkle remaining crumbs evenly over top. Cover and freeze. About 15 minutes before serving, remove from freezer and let set. Cut into 6 pieces.

Serves 6
Each serving equals:
HE: ⅔ Bread, ⅓ Skim Milk, ⅓ Fruit, ¼ Slider, 15 Optional Calories

*Note: The format of this recipe differs from most others in this book at JoAnna Lund's—the author's—request that her original recipe remain exactly as it appeared in her newsletter.

154 Calories, 3 gm Fat, 4 gm Protein, 28 gm Carbohydrate, 226 mg Sodium, 1 gm Fiber
Diabetic: 1 Starch, ½ Fruit, ½ Fat

HINT: Nilla crushed crumbs can be used instead of graham cracker crumbs.

Prune Butter

To make prune butter, place 8 ounces pitted prunes (about 1⅓ cups) and 6 tablespoons water or fruit juice in a food processor. Process at high speed until the mixture is a smooth paste. (Mixture is too thick to be made in a blender.) Use immediately, or place in an airtight container and store for up to 3 weeks in the refrigerator. Yields 1 cup.

Pudding (Chocolate)

Serves 6

Place in a large, heavy-duty saucepan:

**2 cups skim milk
2 cups water
1 cup dry milk powder
⅔ cup sugar
2 tablespoons sifted cocoa**

Mix well with a wire whisk. Turn on medium heat and place pan on hot burner. Stir occasionally. Into a small container, measure and pour:

**¾ cup water
6 tablespoons cornstarch (a little less than ½ cup)**

Put on a tight-fitting lid. Shake container until cornstarch and water are completely mixed, with no lumps. Stir cornstarch mixture into hot milk mixture. Stir constantly for several minutes, until pudding begins to thicken. Cook and stir for another 2 minutes. Remove from heat. Stir in:

1 teaspoon vanilla

Serve hot or cold.

Variations: For vanilla pudding, omit cocoa and ⅛ cup sugar. For banana pudding, add 3 mashed bananas to the vanilla pudding recipe.

Tips: This pudding takes some time, but the taste is so much better than store-bought, it's worth it. Ask one of your older children or your spouse to do the stirring while you cook the rest of the meal.

Nutritional Data for One Serving (1 cup): Calories: 191, Calories from Fat: 4, Total Fat: 0 g, Saturated Fat: 0 g, Cholesterol: 4 mg, Sodium: 109 mg, Total Carbohydrate: 41 g, Dietary Fiber: 0 g, Sugars: 25 g, Protein: 7 g, Vitamin A: 13% RDA, Vitamin C: 2% RDA, Calcium: 25% RDA, Iron: 4% RDA

Smoothie Variation (Like Ice Cream)

Serves 4 to 6

Place in a blender:

1 to 2 cups frozen fruit: bananas, strawberries, blueberries, etc.
½ to 1½ cups of yogurt, milk, and/or fruit juice

Fill the rest of the pitcher with ice. Blend until smooth. Add liquid slowly until desired consistency is reached.

Variations: Try different combinations of fruits, relying most on those in season (and cheapest).

Nutritional Data for One Serving: Too hard to figure.

Strawberry "Pudding"

Serves 8

Adapted from a recipe by Jan Kent, author of
the *A Taste of Dutch* cookbook.

Into a blender, pour:

½ cup water

Sprinkle over the top:

2 envelopes unflavored gelatin

Let stand 3 to 4 minutes. Bring to a boil:

1 cup skim milk

Pour into blender. Process at low speed until gelatin is completely dissolved, about 2 minutes. Add and process at high speed:

⅓ cup sugar
1 teaspoon almond (or vanilla) extract
½ to 1 quart strawberries, stemmed and halved

Pour into dessert dishes or a bowl. Chill until set.

Variations: One teaspoon sugar substitute can be used in place of sugar. Use an equal amount of seasonal fruit or mixed fruit instead of strawberries.

Tips: Be careful not to let the boiling milk overflow and make a mess.

Nutritional Data for One Serving (⅔ cup): Calories: 67, Calories from Fat: 2, Total Fat: 0 g, Saturated Fat: 0 g, Cholesterol: 1 mg, Sodium: 19 mg, Total Carbohydrate: 14 g, Dietary Fiber: 1 g, Sugars: 13 g, Protein: 3 g, Vitamin A: 2% RDA, Vitamin C: 55% RDA, Calcium: 5% RDA, Iron: 2% RDA

Swedish Apple Pudding with Custard Sauce

From *Healthy Exchanges Food Newsletter.**

18 (2½-x-2½-inch) graham crackers
3 cups unsweetened applesauce
1½ teaspoons JO's Apple Pie Spice**
1 (4 serving) package Jell-O sugar-free vanilla cook-and-serve pudding mix
2 cups skim milk
1 teaspoon vanilla extract
1 tablespoon reduced-calorie margarine

Preheat oven to 350 degrees. Place 9 graham crackers in a 9-x-9-inch cake pan. Spoon 1½ cups applesauce over crackers. Sprinkle ½ teaspoon JO's Apple Pie Spice over applesauce. Place 6 crackers evenly over top. Spoon remaining applesauce over crackers and sprinkle with another ½ teaspoon JO's Apple Pie Spice. Crush remaining 3 crackers and sprinkle cracker crumbs evenly over top. Bake 45 minutes. About 10 minutes before apple pudding is done, combine dry pudding mix and skim milk in a medium saucepan. Cook over medium heat, stirring constantly with a wire whisk, until mixture thickens and starts to boil. Remove from heat. Stir in vanilla extract, reduced-calorie margarine, and remaining ½ teaspoon JO's Apple Pie Spice. Let apple pudding cool 2 to 3 minutes. For each serving, place apple pudding on dessert dish and top with ⅓ cup warm custard sauce.

Serves 6
Each serving equals:
HE: 1 Bread, 1 Fruit, ⅓ Skim Milk, 13 Optional Calories
186 Calories, 2 gm Fat, 4 gm Protein, 38 gm Carbohydrate, 281 mg Sodium, 2 gm Fiber
Diabetic: 1½ Starch, 1 Fruit

HINT: (1) Also good with apple pudding cold and sauce warmed in microwave. (2) Substitute any reputable brand for JO's Apple Pie Spice. (3) Two tablespoons chopped walnuts can be sprinkled on top with remaining cracker crumbs.

*Note: The format of this recipe differs from most others in this book at JoAnna Lund's—the author's—request that her original recipe remain exactly as it appeared in her newsletter.
**See Resources under "Miscellaneous Products" for how to order JO's Spices.

Recipe Permissions

Applesauce Gingerbread recipe reprinted with permission from *Secrets of Fat-Free Baking*, by Sandra Woodruff. Copyright 1994, published by Avery Publishing Group, Inc., Garden City Park, New York, 1-800-548-5757.

Bagels recipe reprinted with permission from *Cheap Eating*, by Pat Edwards, Upper Access Books, Copyright 1993, Hinesburg, Vermont, now out of print.

Baked Fruity Chicken recipe reprinted with permission from *The $30 a Week Grocery Budget, Volume I,* by Donna McKenna (author and publisher, no copyright date), Brooklet, Georgia.

Banana-Cranberry Muffins recipe reprinted with permission from *Healthy Exchanges Food Newsletter,* by JoAnna M. Lund (author and publisher). Copyright 1995, DeWitt, Iowa.

Beef and Noodle Soup recipe reprinted with permission from *Healthy Exchanges Food Newsletter,* by JoAnna M. Lund (author and publisher). Copyright 1995, DeWitt, Iowa.

Breakfast Biscuits recipe reprinted with permission from *Healthy Exchanges Food Newsletter,* by JoAnna M. Lund (author and publisher). Copyright 1995, DeWitt, Iowa.

Caramel Apricot Rice Pudding recipe reprinted with permission from *Healthy Exchanges Food Newsletter,* by JoAnna M. Lund (author and publisher). Copyright 1995, DeWitt, Iowa.

Cheesy Tuna Garden Skillet recipe reprinted with permission from *Healthy Exchanges Food Newsletter,* by JoAnna M. Lund (author and publisher). Copyright 1995, DeWitt, Iowa.

Crystallized Grapes and Oranges recipe reprinted with permission from *Cheap Eating,* by Pat Edwards, Upper Access Books, Copyright 1993, Hinesburg, Vermont, now out of print.

Dragon Sauce recipe reprinted with permission from *Dinner's in the Freezer,* by Jill Bond, GCB Publishing, Copyright 1995, Elkton, Maryland, now out of print.

Florida Cracker Lemonade recipe reprinted with permission from *Dinner's in the Freezer,* by Jill Bond, GCB Publishing, Copyright 1995, Elkton, Maryland, now out of print.

French Toast recipe reprinted with permission from *The $30 a Week Grocery Budget, Volume I,* by Donna McKenna (author and publisher, no copyright), Brooklet, Georgia.

Golden Broccoli Salad recipe reprinted with permission from *Healthy Exchanges Food Newsletter,* by JoAnna M. Lund (author and publisher). Copyright 1995, DeWitt, Iowa.

Greek Feta Salad recipe reprinted with permission from *Healthy Exchanges Food Newsletter,* by JoAnna M. Lund (author and publisher). Copyright 1995, DeWitt, Iowa.

PEAK SEASON FOR FRUITS & VEGETABLES

	JANUARY	FEBRUARY	MARCH	APRIL	MAY	JUNE	JULY	AUGUST	SEPTEMBER	OCTOBER	NOVEMBER	DECEMBER
FRUIT												
Apples									▓	▓	▓	▓
Apricot					▓		▓					
Avocados			▓	▓		▓	▓		▓			
Bananas												
Blackberries						▓						
Blueberries							▓					
Cherries						▓						
Cranberries											▓	
Grapefruit	▓	▓									▓	▓
Grapes												
Lemons												
Melons												
Nectarines							▓					
Oranges	▓	▓										▓
Peaches							▓					
Pears								▓	▓			
Pineapples												
Plums				▓								
Raspberries						▓						
Strawberries					▓							
Tangerines	▓											▓
Watermelon					▓							
VEGETABLES												
Artichokes			▓									
Asparagus				▓								
Green Beans						▓		▓				
Beets							▓		▓			
Broccoli	▓									▓	▓	▓
Brussel Sprouts												
Cabbage					▓							
Carrots	▓	▓	▓	▓	▓	▓	▓	▓	▓	▓	▓	▓
Celery	▓	▓										
Corn						▓						
Cucumber						▓						
Eggplant								▓				
Lettuce						▓						
Mushrooms											▓	
Onions					▓							
Green Onions												
Peas				▓					▓			
Peppers								▓				
Potatoes	▓									▓		
Pumpkins										▓		
Spinach			▓									
Tomatoes									▓			
Winter Squash												

Reprinted with permission from *The Frugle Times*, September 1992

CHAPTER 7

A Final Word

As of this writing, we are continuing to budget $12 a day, about $84 a week, for healthy food. Most of the time we're staying within that budget. But some days it seems almost impossible to spend so little. That's when I remind myself of why we limited ourselves in the first place: in order to transfer dollars from grocery bills to higher-priority areas, like better housing and yearly vacations to visit our relatives.

Some weeks I overspend. I get tired of the hassle, I'm not well organized, or I simply want to buy more treats than usual. Although I make mistakes, Michael and I continue to try to contain the dollar amount we've set for groceries. This isn't easy, with four growing children, including two teenage boys, in the house.

On the other hand, I am excited about the information I've been able to share with you in *Feed Your Family for $12 a Day*. A combination of money-saving techniques and hard work is essential if any of us are going to keep our grocery bills at half the national average. But I am convinced this task is not impossible.

Again, $12 a day may be an unrealistic figure for some of you. And perhaps not all of the strategies and cost-cutting ideas apply to your situation; they don't all apply to ours. What I have tried to show is that there are many different approaches to saving money on groceries. I am confident that you will be able to discover what works best for you and adjust your lifestyle accordingly.

A final chapter should point out that this book is certainly not *the* final word. I hope to hear from many of you who are more expert than I am at saving money on food: write and tell me about any good ideas, healthy recipes, or techniques you know—and I don't. (See page 184 for my address and Web site.)

In the meantime, let me leave you with a checklist, a summary of most of the ideas in this book, to encourage you as you tackle the important job of cutting back on your food budget. What could you do, starting today? What could you do next week? Next month?

CHECKLIST FOR SAVINGS

- Set up a budget for groceries and plan to spend that total amount weekly.
- Visit several different stores over a period of a few weeks in order to compare prices.
- Assemble a notebook that lists each store's prices on products you buy regularly.
- Make a detailed, well-planned weekly list.
- Clip coupons and combine them with specials at a double coupon store.
- Watch for good refund offers on foods you buy, then redeem them.
- Look over a refunding magazine to see if large-scale refunding and couponing appeal to you.
- Resolve to shop once a week or less when possible.
- Stick to your list when you shop.
- Eliminate impulse buying.
- Buy generic or store brand products whenever possible.
- Buy in bulk. This may be as simple as stocking up on supermarket specials.
- Utilize the Pantry Principle.
- Buy produce that is currently in season.
- Stock up on fresh, seasonal fruits and vegetables at a pick-your-own place.
- Stock up on candy right after Halloween, Christmas, and other holidays.
- Call around to find alternative food sources in your area.
- Join and shop at a membership warehouse club.
- Shop at a dairy or a cheese outlet.
- Shop at a health food store for some items like spices.
- Shop at a bakery outlet (sometimes called a day-old-bread store).

- Shop at a produce stand.
- Shop at a meat market that offers special values on meat.
- Shop at a farmers' market.
- Try to buy as many foods on sale as possible when you shop at the supermarket.
- Substitute store brand or generic products for name brands.
- Eliminate most convenience foods from your meals.
- Start making some foods, such as salad dressings and croutons, from scratch.
- Bake your own bread, by hand or with a breadmaker.
- Prepare some recipes in large quantities so "convenience foods" are ready in the freezer.
- Make out monthly menu plans.
- Do most of your cooking once every two to four weeks.
- Mega-cook several of the same kinds of meals in large quantities.
- Keep a careful watch of leftovers and use or freeze excess amounts biweekly.
- Resolve to try 24-hour-in-advance meal planning for most efficient use of foods on hand.
- Do 15-minute cooking to save both time and money on healthy meals.
- Substitute a balanced variety of other foods for large helpings of meat.
- Serve smaller portions of expensive foods.
- Serve larger portions of healthy, filling foods like brown rice, beans, and whole-grain breads.
- Replace nonnutritious foods, like sugary desserts and white bread, with nutritious ones, like low-fat custards and whole-wheat bread.
- Substitute less-expensive breakfast items, like oatmeal or toast with all-fruit spread, for doughnuts and fancy cereals.
- Drink water, brewed tea, and fruit juice rather than boxed fruit drinks, coffee, and soda.
- Eat less.
- Brown bag your family's lunches.
- Start a garden.
- Consider becoming a member of a garden club to better learn how to grow your own food.
- If you lack garden space, look into alternatives, such as square foot gardening or planting in containers.

- Visit your library or County Extension Service for free information on gardening, as well as a number of other topics.
- Learn how to preserve your own food through canning, freezing, and other techniques.
- Be on the lookout for gleaning possibilities.
- Barter for food with friends and neighbors.
- Call SHARE headquarters to learn if the organization has a branch in your area.
- Join a commercial bartering exchange, or at least call and find out more.
- Join a cooperative.
- Entertain economically.
- Eat more meals at home.
- Limit the amount of money spent on meals away from home.
- Find out, when absolutely necessary, if your family is eligible for any government programs that help pay for food.
- Read other books or Web sites that will help you save on your grocery bills.
- Remember why you're trimming your grocery bill: to free up extra money so that you can begin to realize some of the dreams in your life.

Nobody will be able to—or want to—do everything on this list, or all that's described in *Feed Your Family for $12 a Day*. But like our hypothetical Price family, implementing one small step at a time can make a significant difference in the amount of money you're spending on groceries. Whatever your food budget, and however you decide to cook, shop, and implement various strategies, may your savings make a positive difference and help you realize the dreams in your life.

Sincerely,
Rhonda Barfield
P.O. Box 665
St. Charles, MO 63303
www.lilacpublishing.com

More Real-Life Shopping Lists and Menu Plans

One week's shopping list and menu plans are described in Chapter 1. For those of you who want to know more about how I shop and cook, here are two additional, consecutive weeks of actual lists and the menus that followed.

SHOPPING LIST, WEEK #2

Aldi

5 pounds flour	$ .69
4 pounds white sugar	1.29
2 18-ounce boxes cornflakes	1.78
19-ounce box frosted shredded wheat	1.69
2 18-ounce boxes bran flakes with raisins	2.58
42-ounce box quick oats	1.29
4 pounds powdered milk	6.99
8 ounces Parmesan cheese	1.99
16-ounce package all-purpose crackers	.99
16-ounce box saltines	.49
15-ounce package tortilla chips	.89
2 13-ounce cans potato chips	1.89
13-ounce package crunchy cheese curls	.89
26 ounces spaghetti sauce	.99
15 ounces raisins	.99

16 ounces peanuts	$1.69
2 3-ounce boxes strawberry gelatin	.50
1 pound strawberries	1.49
10 pounds bananas	2.51
16-ounce package lettuce salad	.79
15-ounce can green beans	.29
15-ounce can peas	.29
15-ounce can pork and beans	.29
1 gallon 2% milk	2.18
1 gallon skim milk	1.89
2 dozen eggs	.98
1 pound margarine	.49
6 8-ounce containers fruit yogurt	2.34
16 ounces grated mozzarella cheese	2.49
3 12-ounce packages turkey lunch meat	.87
4.6 pounds frozen whole chicken	2.75
2 8-packs hamburger buns	.78
1 8-pack hot dog buns	.39
12-ounce orange juice concentrate	.69
2 12-ounce grape juice concentrate	1.38
6 ice cream sandwiches	1.69
8-ounce container whipped topping	.69
Total, with tax:	$52.96

Mid-Towne IGA

8 ounces plain yogurt	$ .89
10 ounces marshmallows	1.11
5 pounds whole-wheat flour	2.39
14-ounce package fat-free hot dogs	3.75
Total, with tax:	$8.50

Vaccaro & Sons Produce

1 cantaloupe	$ .99
5 yellow apples	1.51
2 tomatoes	.69
2½ pounds red grapes	2.66
5 pounds peaches	2.99
1 watermelon	2.67

Damaged Produce	$2.00
3 pounds onions	
15 pounds potatoes	
2 cartons blueberries	
7 ears of corn	
1 yellow pepper	
Total, with tax:	$14.09

Quik Trip	
1 gallon 2% milk	$2.66
Grand Total, Week #2:	*$78.21*

This week I shopped at Aldi as usual. Its private label mozzarella cheese, packaged in 16-ounce bags, is actually cheaper per ounce than a co-op's bulk buy cheese. The same is true of Aldi's pretzels in 12-ounce bags; they're cheaper than Sam's Club's version. This was one of the surprising discoveries I made when first comparing prices.

When given the opportunity, I usually buy damaged fruits and vegetables at the produce stand along with my regular purchases. For the most part, fruits have one small bruise or cut, lettuce is slightly wilted, and bananas are at peak ripeness: this is the sort of produce that is, unfortunately, often thrown away. I appreciate the chance to prevent the waste of good food as well as to feed my family more nutritionally.

Because we own one small refrigerator, I usually purchase only a couple of gallons of milk at Aldi each week. When needed, one of my children can walk a block to the local QT to buy another gallon for about 50 cents more than Aldi's price. To me, the two quarters spent are well worth the convenience of more room in the fridge.

Notice that I'm under budget this week. I had to make up for the extra expense last week!

MENUS, WEEK #2

Monday
    Breakfast: Choice of granola,* cornflakes, instant oatmeal, and/or fresh fruit, milk; Eric usually eats two bowls of bran

flakes cereal and a cup of store-bought yogurt each
morning

Lunch: Lunch meat sandwiches, choice of fruit, graham
crackers

Dinner: Salmon croquettes,* corn muffins,* lettuce salad,
Lemon Gelatin Delight*

Tuesday
Breakfast: Toast, eggs, fruit, milk
Lunch: Pasta with vegetarian spaghetti sauce and cheese, corn
chips, choice of fruit (grapes, apples, cantaloupe)
Dinner: Grilled hamburgers and hot dogs, French fries,* corn
on the cob, relish tray (sliced tomatoes, onions, and lettuce leaves), diced strawberries, ice cream sandwiches

Wednesday
Breakfast: Shredded wheat and/or cornflakes, milk
Lunch: (Leftover) hot dogs, potato chips, choice of fruit
Snack: Mary's treat of chocolate cake, stack of crackers, grapes
on toothpicks, and fruit punch
Dinner: Hashbrown potatoes* with (leftover) grilled burgers (in
chunks), leftover corn muffins,* whole-grain bread,
canned peas, maple waldorf apple salad*

Thursday
Breakfast: Choice of granola,* cornflakes, instant oatmeal, and/or
fresh fruit, milk
Lunch: Beef and noodle soup,* snack crackers, choice of fruit
Dinner: Haystacks,* rice, popovers,* lettuce salad, carrot coins

Friday
Breakfast: Choice of granola,* cornflakes, instant oatmeal, and/or
fresh fruit, milk
Lunch: Macaroni and cheese, popovers* (leftover), choice of
fruit; I ate the last of the red beans and rice
Dinner: Baked fruity chicken,* homemade biscuits, boiled eggs,
fruit salad,* chocolate cake (leftover)

Saturday
Breakfast: Oatmeal pancakes,* milk

Lunch: Cheese tortillas, cheese curls, watermelon slices

Dinner: Pork and chicken in barbecue sauce,* on homemade French bread,* lettuce leaves, sliced tomatoes, diced hard-boiled eggs, easy baked beans,* sliced fresh peaches, watermelon

Sunday

Breakfast: Choice of granola,* cornflakes, instant oatmeal, pancakes, and/or fresh fruit, milk

Lunch: Lunch out at friends' house

Dinner: Hazel's Five-Hour Stew,* French bread (leftover),* fresh blueberries, cantaloupe

On Saturday I decided it was time to make room in the refrigerator and freezer. The evening meal featured several leftover dishes set out on the table like a mini-buffet. You may notice we also serve leftovers for lunches. Some of our children prefer freshly prepared foods, and we give them the option of making themselves a pb&j sandwich instead.

My daughter Mary, age ten, is an excellent cook. On Wednesday, she held an afternoon tea party for one of her stuffed animals, hence the special foods. Mary prepared a cake from scratch, baked it, made icing, and frosted the cooled cake. Days like these make me glad I took the time, when she was younger, to teach her to cook.

Our neighbor Diana started a high-protein diet last week and wanted to get rid of several boxes of pasta, which she gave to us. Some of the pasta was served in two lunches of beef and noodle soup and macaroni and cheese. We also ate more lettuce salad than usual because I found several heads at the produce stand in the "damaged" box. I try to take and use any extra food that's made available to my family.

SHOPPING LIST, WEEK #3

Aldi

5 pounds flour	$.69
4 pounds sugar	1.29
2 pounds powdered sugar	.89

2 pounds brown sugar	.89
24 ounces pancake syrup	.89
12-ounce can evaporated milk	.49
18-ounce chocolate cake mix	.69
18-ounce box cornflakes	.89
18-ounce box sugar-frosted wheat puffs	1.69
2 18-ounce boxes bran flakes with raisins	2.58
42-ounce box quick oats	1.29
16-ounce package snack crackers	.99
15-ounce package nacho cheese chips	.89
15-ounce package tortilla chips	.89
2 13-ounce cans potato chips	1.89
26 ounces spaghetti sauce	.99
18 ounces peanut butter	1.29
24 ounces honey	1.79
1 pound mixed nuts	1.99
16-ounce box vanilla wafers	.89
16 ounces baby carrots	.99
16-ounce package lettuce salad	.79
29-ounce can peaches	.79
20-ounce can pineapple	.59
15-ounce can beans	.39
14-ounce can spinach	.39
15-ounce can peas	.29
16-ounce jar sweet pickles	.99
24-ounce jar salsa	1.49
28-ounce bottle ketchup	.69
1¼-ounce package taco seasoning	.29
2½-ounce onion soup mix	.49
1 gallon 2% milk	2.18
16 ounces grated cheddar cheese	2.49
16 ounces grated mozzarella cheese	2.49
24 ounces low-fat cottage cheese	1.49
1 pound margarine	.49
12-ounce package turkey lunch meat	1.69
24 ounces frozen whiting filets	2.89
8-pack hot dog buns	.39
20-ounce loaf wheat bread	.69
12-ounce apple juice concentrate	.69
2 12-ounce orange juice concentrate	1.38

12-ounce grape juice concentrate	.69
6 ice cream sandwiches	1.99
Total, with tax:	$51.41

Mid-Towne IGA

1 pound lasagna noodles	$1.47
2 pounds popcorn	1.29
14-ounce package fat-free hot dogs	3.75
2 1-pound packages frozen ground turkey	2.38
2.8 pounds split chicken breasts	3.64
Total, with tax:	$13.07

Vaccaro & Sons Produce

2 cantaloupes	$3.00
1 head lettuce	.89
4 peaches	1.51
4 perfect apples	1.58
5 tomatoes	2.00
6 ears of corn	1.49

Damaged Produce:	$2.00
Several spears asparagus	
21 bananas	
32 red and yellow apples	
Total, with tax:	$12.92

Pepperidge Farms Bread Store

| 4 24-ounce loaves whole-grain bread | $3.98 |

Quik Trip

| 1 gallon 2% milk | $2.66 |

| *Grand Total, Week #3:* | *$84.04* |

I buy a great deal of produce, as you can see. Most of it we eat each week. The children are almost always welcome to go to the cupboard and eat as much fresh fruit as they want. If fresh fruit is running low, I try to have fruit ice pops available in the freezer.

You may wonder, looking over the shopping lists, how we stretch so little meat for six people. The answer is that we serve small amounts of meat and larger amounts of more filling foods.

Remember also that I work to keep a surplus of food in the cupboards, freezer, and refrigerator rather than using up everything and starting over each week.

MENUS, WEEK #3

Monday
Breakfast: Choice of granola,* cornflakes, instant oatmeal, pancakes, and/or fresh fruit, milk; Eric usually eats two bowls of bran flakes cereal and a cup of store-bought yogurt each morning

Lunch: Tortilla chips and melted cheese, grapes, bananas

Dinner: Hamburger stroganoff,* pasta, green beans, banana bread,* apple crisp* with whipped topping*

Tuesday
Breakfast: French toast,* milk

Lunch: Choice of tuna salad* or peanut butter and jelly sandwiches on whole-grain bread, apples, oranges

Dinner: Momwiches* and hot dogs, scalloped potatoes,* relish tray of sliced tomatoes, onions, and lettuce leaves; banana salad

Wednesday
Breakfast: Sugared wheat puffs, milk

Lunch: Choice of tuna salad* or hot dogs (leftover), cheese curls, bananas

Dinner: Baked chicken breasts, scalloped potatoes* (leftover), poppy seed muffins,* apple slices

Thursday
Breakfast: Choice of granola,* cornflakes, instant oatmeal, and/or fresh fruit, milk

Lunch: Stir-fry* (ground turkey, yellow pepper, and onion) on pasta, bananas and apples

Dinner: Grilled chicken breasts, stuffing* with low-fat gravy, green beans, gelatin salad with bananas,* orange sherbet*

Friday

Breakfast: Choice of granola,* cornflakes, instant oatmeal, pancakes, and/or fresh fruit, milk

Lunch: Grilled cheese sandwiches, cheese curls, choice of fresh fruit

Dinner: Steamed fish,* pumpkin muffins* and banana bread* (from the freezer), leftovers from last night, frozen fruit delight*

Saturday

Breakfast: Oatmeal pancakes*, milk

Lunch (with friends): Lasagna,* French bread,* lettuce and tomato salad

Dinner: Baked chicken,* homemade rolls, corn on the cob, fruit salad*

Sunday

Breakfast: Cold cereal with milk

Lunch: Take-out pizza, lettuce salad, carrots, fresh fruit salad

Dinner (a birthday cookout at the lake with relatives):

Hot dogs, potato chips, apple slices, homemade cake

* Starred items can be found in the Recipe Index. Look them up; you'll be surprised at the low-fat content.

Remember, again, that I don't always design the most creative menus. Notice that on both Wednesday and Thursday evening I served chicken breasts, and then we had baked chicken on Sunday. I often plan better than this, but my husband and/or children may overrule me if a particular dish sounds good to them. Also, as was mentioned earlier, if I get a great deal on a particular kind of fruit or vegetable, we eat quite a lot of it.

We served hot dogs, a favorite summer food, more often this week than we should have. This is an example of one of those times when we begin to move away from healthy foods, then have to get back on track later.

You may recall that I often bake and cook ahead, and this week I took advantage of some of my surplus. Pumpkin muffins, banana bread, and dry bread for stuffing, as listed in this week's menus, all came from the freezer. We often have extra sliced onions after a barbecue, and I dice them and freeze them in a zippered bag, ready to add to dishes like soups. Most Saturday mornings, I cook a huge batch of oatmeal pancakes and freeze about half to have on hand for other breakfasts during the week.

On Monday, Mary and Lisa made grape juice ice pops and ate several for snacks over the next few days. I have help not only with occasional snacks and desserts, but also with dinner every night. Eric, Christian, Lisa, and Mary take turns being "Junior Chef." One person helps me get something started in early morning, and another helps with more involved kitchen duties in late afternoon. This not only makes my job much easier, it also makes it more enjoyable.

Some of you may wonder, with these lists of basic, "unprepared" foods, if I spend all my time in the kitchen. Actually, cooking is rather low on my priority list compared to homeschooling and working at my business. Leftovers and goods from the freezer are my "convenience foods." I also rely heavily on fast, easy recipes. That's why our breakfasts ordinarily require 5 to 10 minutes' preparation; lunches, the same; and dinners, 15 to 40 minutes. It's a rare day when I'm cooking in the kitchen for more than 1½ hours, total.

I hope these additional shopping lists and menus have been helpful to you. May they inspire you to feed your family perfectly nutritional foods (even better than my menus) and to do so as economically as possible.

RESOURCES

Books and Booklets

Ball Blue Book Guide to Home Canning, Freezing, and Dehydration

Pick up a copy of this book at Wal-Mart or selected hardware and grocery stores—wherever Ball products are sold. You'll learn all the basics you need to know about preserving food. Published by Altrista Corporation.

Cheap Eating

Pat Edwards describes her book as a way to "feed your family well and spend less." *Cheap Eating* (© 1993, Upper Access Books) goes into more detail than *Eat Healthy* on growing and preserving your own food, plus other money-saving tips and strategies. There are also several excellent low-cost recipes.

The Complete Cheapskate

Mary Hunt's book (© 1998, Broadman and Holman), an updated and blended version of her first two classic books, teaches how to get out of debt, stay out of debt, and break free from money worries forever. Available in bookstores.

DC Super Heroes Super Healthy Cookbook

Mark Saltzman, Judy Garlan, and Michele Grodner have compiled a 100-page classic cookbook of "good food kids can make themselves." Full-color photographs, easy instructions, and superhero cartoons on nearly every page inspire young cooks to head for the kitchen. Though no longer in print, your local library may either have a copy on hand or be able to locate one through interlibrary loan. (While you're looking, browse through other children's cookbooks.)

15-Minute Cooking

Rhonda Barfield's book describes her own system of cooking in just two 15-minute sessions daily, one in the morning and one just before dinner. You'll read about four weeks of typical, easy menu plans, as well as all the details you'll need to create your own. There are also dozens of new recipes, ones that aren't included in this book. Learn how to alternate these recipes (and your own), save money, cut your preparation time to the minimum, and still serve really tasty, home-cooked meals every day. $12.95 including p&h, © 1996, Lilac Publishing. To order, write to Rhonda at her company, Lilac Publishing, P.O. Box 665, St. Charles, MO 63302-0665. Or visit the family Web site at www.lilacpublishing.com.

Food—Your Miracle Medicine: How Food Can Prevent and Cure Over 100 Symptoms and Problems

I've checked out this book from the library so many times I've nearly worn it out. Jean Carper, author and medical researcher, cites hundreds of scientific studies on foods that are particularly heatlthy. Fascinating reading, this book (© 1998, HarperCollins) really helped motivate us to eat better. Available in bookstores.

Gardening by Mail: A Sourcebook

Barbara J. Barton's detailed sourcebook (© 1986, Houghton Mifflin) lists all kinds of gardening supplies available through mail-order. You'll find this book in most bookstores.

Healthy Exchanges Cookbooks

JoAnna M. Lund, author, describes her numerous collections as "common folk" healthy cookbooks. If you tried the mouth-watering sugar-free, low-fat, low-sodium recipes I borrowed with JoAnna's permission, I'm sure you know what she means. Call 1-800-766-8961 for credit card orders and current prices or visit her Web site at www.healthyexchanges.com. JoAnna will tell you about her books as well as her newsletter of the same name.

Invest in Yourself: Six Secrets to a Rich Life

This book by Marc Eisenson, Gerry Detweiler, and Nancy Castleman (© 1998, John Wiley & Sons) is an excellent introduction to determining priorities, going after personal goals, and getting the most for your money. Find out what you can do with all the money you've saved on groceries, and improve your life as you invest in yourself! It's offered in bookstores nationwide in both paperback and hardback. For more information, visit www.goodadvicepress.com.

Mega-Cooking

A 446-page hardback, *Mega-Cooking* (© 2000, Cumberland House Publishing) is a comprehensive home-management system with detailed information on pre-preparing food. Jill Bond, author, shares her expertise as a mega-cook who often prepares up to six months' worth of economical, nutritious meals. Available through bookstores.

More-with-Less Cookbook

Doris Janzen Longacre's timeless cookbook is subtitled "Suggestions by Mennonites on how to eat better and consume less of the world's limited food resources." Sold in Christian bookstores (© 2000, Herald Press).

The New Enchanted Broccoli Forest and Other Timeless Delicacies

Mollie Katzen wrote a 320-page vegetarian cookbook in 1982 that "veggie" friends of mine cite as one of their all-time favorites, and this is a recent update (© 2000, Ten Speed Press). Available in bookstores.

Once-a-Month Cooking

Written by Mimi Wilson and Mary Beth Lagerborg, *Once-a-Month Cooking* (© 1999, St. Martin's Press) describes "A Time-Saving, Budget-Stretching Plan to Prepare Delicious Meals." Detailed menus and shopping lists tell all you need to know for shopping and meal preparation, two to four weeks at a time. You'll find it in most bookstores.

Ortho's All About Vegetables

Here's a comprehensive publication, sold in retail stores and bookstores nationwide, that's all about vegetables and how to grow them (© 1998, Ortho).

Ortho Problem Solver

This huge, encyclopedic resource volume contains, among many other features, a listing of every County Extension Service (CES) in the United States. You'll also want to refer to it for answers to over 2,000 gardening problems, especially those related to pests and diseases. Photos illustrate each section. You can find Ortho Problem Solver at many home and garden centers and some hardware stores (© 1999, Meredith Books).

Putting Food By

Janet Greene has assembled a comprehensive book of 512 pages that tells you all you need to know about preserving your food. Available in major bookstores (© 1992, Viking Penguin).

Saving Money Any Way You Can

Here's a fast-paced book that covers nearly every imaginable money-saving topic. You'll find Mike Yorkey's informative volume in Christian bookstores, or order through the publisher at Box 8617, Ann Arbor, Michigan, 48107, 1-800-458-8505 (© 1994, Servant Publications).

Secrets of Fat-Free Baking

I reprinted two recipes from this delightful book in my recipes section (with permission, of course). Sandra Woodruff's creations taste delicious, even without the fat. Available in bookstores (© 1994 Avery Publishing).

Square Foot Gardening

Mel Bartholomew's 347-page book shows you how to make the most of your garden space. This system seems both do-able and sensible, and the author gets you excited about trying. Highly recommended by gardeners I know. Sold in home and garden centers and bookstores (© 1981, Rodale Press).

A Taste of Dutch

This small cookbook contains several tasty recipes from a mother of ten children. Jan Kent charges only $3.50 plus $1.00 p&h for her self-published gem. Send your order to Jan at 1748 Spreckelmeyer Road, Berger, MO 63014. Self-published, 1993.

Thrifty Business: 111 Money-Saving Tips

Rhonda Barfield's *classic* booklet, 32 pages, tells you how to save on groceries, supplies, clothes, some major household purchases, and recreation. The $5.00 price includes postage and handling, plus a guarantee that you'll save at least $50 or your money back. Send a check or money order to TB, P.O. Box 665, St. Charles, MO 63302-0665. Self-published.

Thw $30 a Week Grocery Budget, Volume I
The $30 a Week Grocery Budget, Volume II

Donna McKenna's first volume (60 pages) sells for $5.50; the second, slightly shorter, volume for $5.00, postage and handling included—or $10.00 for both booklets. The first booklet contains detailed information on how Donna feeds a family of six for $30 a week; the second, more general advice on saving money. Both self-published books are worth the price if only for the low-cost recipes. Write to Donna at P.O. Box 391, Brooklet, GA 30415.

The Tightwad Gazette: Promoting Thrift as a Viable Alternative Lifestyle

The first two years of the premiere newsletter (now out of print) by Amy Dacyczyn are condensed into book form. Chock-full of great information, including ideas on saving money on groceries, *The Tightwad Gazette* is available in bookstores (© 1993, Villard Books).

The Tightwad Gazette II
The Tightwad Gazette III

These two volumes contain the next few years of the newsletter by the same name, with the same author (© 1995, 1997, Villard Books).

The Use-It-Up Cookbook

Lois Carlson Willand has written 190 pages, a "Guide for Mini-mizing Food Waste" that shows how to creatively recycle every food imaginable. Send $14.95 (tax and postage included) to Practical Cookbooks, 145 Malcolm Avenue S.E., Minneapolis, MN 55414. Self-published, © 1990.

Whole Foods for the Whole Family Cookbook

Edited by Roberta Bishop Johnson for La Leche League International, this is one of the best, most practical cookbooks featuring whole foods on the market. To order, call 1-800-525-3243 (© 1993, La Leche League).

Food Stores

Aldi Inc.

As of this writing, there are approximately 590 Aldi stores nation-wide, primarily in midwestern states but also expanding as far south and east as South Carolina and Tennessee and as far north as Michigan. To find the store nearest you, check out www.aldi.com on-line, or call national headquarters in Batavia, Illinois (630-879-8100). Note: individual Aldi stores' numbers are *not listed* in local phone books.

Save-A-Lot Food Stores

This food chain is similar to Aldi, but sometimes carries a larger se-lection of foods than Aldi does and is located in some areas where Aldi is not. Currently there are more than 900 stores, some independ-ently owned, and others, corporate stores, in thirty-three states total. Save-A-Lot stores are located as far south as Florida and as far west as California. To learn whether or not there is a Save-A-Lot near you, consult the white pages of your phone directory.

Membership Warehouse Clubs

To find a membership warehouse club, pick up your telephone white pages and check under one of the following companies' names, then call one of their numbers. Or visit the Web sites listed below.

BJ's Wholesale Club
Call 1-800-BJS CLUB or visit online at www.bjs.com.

Costco Wholesale
Call 1-800-774-2678 or visit online at www.costco.com.

Sam's Wholesale Club
Call 1-800-925-6278 or visit online www.samsclub.com.

Miscellaneous Products

Beating the High Cost of Eating (VHS) Video
Barbara Salsbury, originator of THE PANTRY PRINCIPLE, explains how to save big money at the grocery store and at home in this excellent 95-minute video (awarded four stars by ABC CLEO Video Rating Guide for Libraries). To order both the video and a 76-page worksheet packet (a $10 value, free), mail $19.95 plus $5.00 s&h to Salsbury Enterprises, 9198 Tortellini Drive, Sandy, UT 84093. For credit card orders, call 1-800-619-3821 or visit Barbara's Web site at www.preparednessonline.com.

JO's Spices
JoAnna Lund (of *Healthy Exchanges* fame) has created a collection of seasoning blends containing no salt, sugar, wheat, or MSG. For information, call JO's Spices, 1-800-766-8961.

Sarah Crain Enterprises
Sarah Crain sells a complete breadmaking system including the BOSCH Universal Kitchen Center, along with the lifetime-guaranteed Grainmaster Whisper Mill, books, breadmaker accessories, grain and other consumables, and much more. E-mail Sarah at scrain@home-schoolplanbook.com for more information, or call 636-338-9218.

Newsletters

Cheapskate Monthly
Mary Hunt writes an excellent newsletter that focuses on getting out—and staying out—of debt, based on Mary's personal experience. For a one-year subscription, send $18 plus $4.95 p&h to *Cheapskate*

Monthly, P.O. Box 2135, Paramount, CA 90723-8135 (cash, check, or money order only).

Healthy Exchanges Newsletter

JoAnna Lund, author of the *Healthy Exchanges* cookbooks, also writes a monthly newsletter filled with delicious no-sugar, low-fat, low-sodium recipes and good advice. Send $22.50 for twelve issues to *Healthy Exchanges*, P.O. Box 80, DeWitt, IA 52742-0080, call 1-800-766-8961 for credit card orders, or visit her Web site at www.healthy exchanges.com.

The Pocket Change Investor

This is a quarterly newsletter dedicated to helping readers save money on their debts, like credit card bills and mortgages. A one-year subscription (four issues) costs $12.95. Send payment to Good Advice Press, Box 78, Elizaville, NY 12523. Or visit publishers Nancy Castleman and Marc Eisenson's Web site at www.goodadvicepress.com.

Refund Express

If you're interested in large-scale couponing and refunding, send $4.25 for a sample issue of the *Refund Express* newsletter to P.O. Box 179, Commerce, GA 30529, or check out www.refundexpress.net.

Refunding Newsletters Online

Using a search engine, type in the key word "refunding" to find a listing of refunding newsletters available online.

Organizations and More

The American Dietetic Association's National Center For Nutrition and Dietetics

The Consumer Nutrition Hot Line, 1-800-366-1655, is a service where consumers may call, Monday through Friday, 8 A.M. to 8 P.M. (CST) to listen to recorded messages on current nutrition topics in Spanish and English. To visit the Web site, go to www.eatright.org.

Cooperative Extension Service

This division of the U.S. Department of Agriculture provides all sorts of free and low-cost services to local citizens. To contact a

Cooperative Extension Service in your area, first check the phone directory under "Extension Service." If that doesn't help, try a subheading under "County Agencies." Or contact your local state university (CES is associated with each state's land-grant college or university; in Illinois, it's University of Illinois, for example, and the University of Missouri in my home state). If all else fails, go to a local home and garden center and take a look at *Ortho Problem Solver*, a huge resource book listing every CES in the United States.

La Leche League

For information on breast-feeding and help in locating a nearby chapter, visit online at www.lalecheleague.org.

Library System

If you cannot find a book (or other material) at the local library, request an interlibrary loan. Staff members will first try to locate a copy of your request in libraries nearby, then within your county or state. Depending on the circumstances, they may even make a nationwide search if necessary. Usually there is only a small fee involved, and sometimes the search is free.

Another option is to ask your library to buy a particular book (video, CD, etc.). Libraries are often very open to customer requests and will do their best to accommodate you. To ensure an even better chance that your request is honored, ask one or two friends to call and ask for the same item.

National Commercial Exchange

To learn more about commercial bartering exchanges, visit NCE's Web site at www.ncebarter.com.

National Cooperative Business Association

For a free information packet on cooperatives and up-to-date information on cooperatives in your area, visit NCBA at www.ncba.org, or e-mail ncba@ncba.org.

National Council of State Garden Clubs

Visit the council's Web site at www.gardenclub.org, or call 314-776-7574 for information on the club nearest you in your state.

Share (Self Help and Resource Exchange)
This is the organization that offers discounted packages of groceries to qualified groups whose individuals work public service hours. Headquartered in San Diego, California, SHARE is currently located in several regions across the United States. To discover whether or not there's a SHARE near you, call 1-888-742-7372; if you get a response, there is a group operating in your area; if no response, no affiliate is nearby.

U.S. Cooperative Food Warehouses
The National Cooperative Business Association currently lists the following contacts as regional sources for co-op buying. If you find an address or phone number is no longer correct, please contact the NCBA for up-to-date information.

National
Frontier Natural Products Co-op
Box 299
Norway, IA 52318
319-227-7991
Serves the nation with herbs and spices

Regional Co-ops (in alphabetical order)

Blooming Prairie Natural Foods
510 Kasota Avenue, SE
Minneapolis, MN 55414
612-378-9774
Serves IA, IL, KS, MI, MN, MO, NE, ND, SD, WI

Federation of Ohio River Cooperatives
320-E Outerbelt, Suite E
Columbus, OH 43213
614-861-2446
Serves IN, KY, MD, MI, NC, OH, PA, SC, VA, WV

North Farm Co-op Warehouse
204 Regas Road
Madison, WI 53714

608-241-2667 or 1-800-236-5880
Serves IL, IN, MI, MN, WI, and parts of IA, MO, MT, ND, OH, SD, WY

Northeast Cooperatives, Inc.
P.O. Box 8188, 49 Bennett Drive
Brattleboro, VT 05304
1-800-334-9939
Serves CT, DC, MA, NH, NJ, NY, PA, RI, VT

Ozark Co-op Warehouse
Box 1528
Fayetteville, AR 72702
501-521-4920
Serves AL, AR, FL, GA, KS, LA, MO, MS, OK, TN, TX

Tucson Cooperative Warehouse
350 S. Toole
Tucson, AZ 85701
520-884-9951
Serves AZ, southern CA, CO, NM, NV, TX, UT

Food Guide Pyramid
A Guide to Daily Food Choices

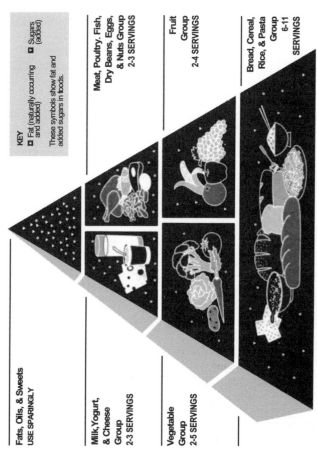

KEY

◻ Fat (naturally occurring and added)   ◼ Sugars (added)

These symbols show fat and added sugars in foods.

Fats, Oils, & Sweets
USE SPARINGLY

Milk, Yogurt, & Cheese Group
2-3 SERVINGS

Meat, Poultry, Fish, Dry Beans, Eggs, & Nuts Group
2-3 SERVINGS

Vegetable Group
2-5 SERVINGS

Fruit Group
2-4 SERVINGS

Bread, Cereal, Rice, & Pasta Group
6-11 SERVINGS

Source: U.S. Department of Agriculture/U.S. Department of Health and Human Services

RECIPE INDEX